From Blah to Awe

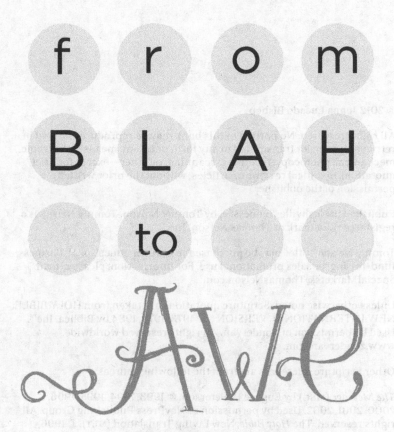

from BLAH to AWE

Shaking Up a Boring Faith

Jenna Lucado Bishop

THOMAS NELSON
Since 1798

NASHVILLE DALLAS MEXICO CITY RIO DE JANEIRO

Published in Nashville, Tennessee, by Tommy Nelson. Tommy Nelson is a registered trademark of Thomas Nelson, Inc.

Tommy Nelson® titles may be purchased in bulk for educational, business, fund-raising, or sales promotional use. For information, please e-mail SpecialMarkets@ThomasNelson.com.

Library of Congress Cataloging-in-Publication Data

Bishop, Jenna Lucado.
From blah to awe : shaking up a boring faith / Jenna Lucado Bishop.
p. cm.
ISBN 978-1-4003-1655-7 (pbk.)
1. Christian teenagers—Religious life. 2. Christian life. 3. Boredom—Religious aspects—Christianity. I. Title.
BV4531.3.B56 2012
248.8'3—dc23 2011035428

Printed in the United States of America

12 13 14 15 QG 6 5 4 3 2 1

For my husband, Brett.

You see the world with a childlike wonder. No matter how many times you have driven down the same West Texas road, your eyes sparkle at its beauty as if you had never seen it before. No matter how many times you have tasted your mom's enchiladas, your mouth smiles as if it were your first taste. And no matter how many times you have watched me sleepily stumble into the kitchen in the morning, your arms wrap around me as if you had never held me before.

The way you see Jesus is no different. No matter how many times you have seen His mercy, tasted His faithfulness, and watched His miracles, your eyes continue to sparkle at His beauty, your mouth continues to smile at His goodness, and your arms continue to stretch toward Him as if you were beholding Him for the first time. Your childlike faith inspired this book.

Contents

PART 1

Why Do I Get Bored with God?

1

Blah, Blah, Blah

Abby

The room was dark.

There were two catwalks.

At the end of each catwalk stood two poles.

Abby knew what they were for, and her stomach knotted. She had heard that these places exist but had never seen one up close. The room felt eerie. What was she doing here?

She had seen the woman standing outside the nightclub. And unlike the thousands of vendors selling food and tourist trinkets on the streets of Antigua, Guatemala, this woman was selling something more valuable—herself. If only the woman knew her true value.

That's why sixteen-year-old Abby had decided to walk across the street to the nightclub entrance where she now stood peering in. She hadn't thought twice about it. This woman needed to know that she was worth more than the fee men paid to use her—a fee that easily could have been as little as two to four dollars an hour.

Abby, along with some others from her mission team, had walked into to the nightclub and asked the owner if they could buy a prostitute for an hour—an hour they hoped would change her life.

Abby always thought of herself as just a "normal" girl. She used to think her story was "boring"—to use her own word. Nothing drastic happened in her life. She didn't struggle with drugs, alcohol, or lots of boy drama. She grew up in a Christian home, attended a Christian school.

So how in the world did this "normal," "boring" girl end up on the streets of Guatemala in the middle of a nightclub full of prostitutes? Because of a very *un*boring, *ab*normal faith.

That faith led Abby to go on a mission trip to Guatemala, which then took her to the scene in our story—a smoke- and lust-filled room. Since it wasn't a busy time, the nightclub owner said they could hang out with one of the prostitutes for free, so he introduced them to Karen.

Karen had no idea why this group of young women was asking her to spend time with them. They definitely weren't her normal customers. She watched them warily as she walked across the street with the group and sat down on a park bench.

Through their translator, the team found out that Karen had three children and that she regularly sold her body to provide food and shelter for her family. Abby's heart broke as she listened to Karen's story of imprisonment to prostitution.

Karen truly believed there was no way out. She had turned to using drugs to numb the pain.

That's when Abby shared her "boring" testimony. You see, a few months prior to the trip, Abby had lost her aunt to a drug overdose. Through tears, Abby told Karen that she didn't want her to die like her aunt, to waste her life. "God loves you," Abby told her. "And through Jesus you *can* have a new life." Then Abby placed a New Testament Bible in Karen's hands.

After talking with Karen about her faith—reassuring her that God loves her and has a plan for her life—Abby decided to pull out her wallet. Although Karen's "owner" had given Karen away for free, Abby, along with her friend Nancy, used up all the cash they had in their wallets to give Karen the money she needed to pay for her children's basic needs. Perhaps their money would lead to one less day of Karen devaluing her body. And maybe one day was all it would take for Karen to find the faith to leave her life of prostitution.

We don't know what happened to Karen after the group of "strange" American women said good-bye to her. Maybe that day changed her life, maybe it didn't. But we do know that day changed Abby's life—forever.

Abby came home with a new excitement about Jesus. Although she had been a Christian a long time, through her experience in Gautemala, Abby discovered a new side of God's heart. "I saw how big God is, how compassionate He is, how much He loves His people."

Abby's faith adventure was just beginning.

Abby, along with her friend Nancy, who had stood with her that afternoon on the streets of Guatemala, sensed that God wanted to use them to build an awareness of women trapped in sex slavery. The hopelessness that Abby and Nancy had seen in Karen's eyes drove them to do something about women who have no choice, women who are stolen, women who are forced into brothels and raped multiple times a day. This devastating reality is called sex trafficking, and it's not limited to Guatemala. It has evolved into an underground, booming business all over the world. And that's why these two teenage girls created SOS223—which stands for "Save Our Sisters" and is based on Jeremiah 22:3: "This is what the LORD says: Do what is fair and right. Save the one who has been robbed from the power of his attacker. Don't mistreat or hurt the foreigners, orphans, or widows. Don't kill innocent people here" (NCV).

They hope to one day make it a legal nonprofit, but for now SOS223 is a title for their efforts. Both have spoken at their high schools about the tragedy of sex trafficking and have raised money to give to established nonprofits that work with victimized women.

Abby says the key to an adventurous faith is serving others. "I feel the closest to God and get so much joy when I'm serving others."

I don't know about you, but I want that kind of faith! A faith that isn't afraid to approach a prostitute and tell her about Jesus. A faith that plants dreams in my heart to change the world, like Abby's dream to end sex trafficking. And a faith that actually acts upon those dreams, believing that God wants to use me. He has a calling on my life. I only need to respond.

Becky

I don't know what Becky loves more—Starbucks' Frappuccinos or smiling.

Frappuccinos I can understand. She and I found out we both share that love as we sat at a Starbucks in San Antonio, Texas—home to both of us.

But smiling? Why would Becky love to smile? When I first met Becky in that Starbucks, I didn't think she had much to smile about. After all, when you are a paraplegic and have been confined to a wheelchair your entire life, wouldn't you feel a little hopeless, depressed, angry at God? Wouldn't you find it hard to smile?

Although Becky admits to questioning God about her condition at times, she chooses to trust a loving God—a God who has given her a purpose, a God who sees more than she does—and her faith outweighs the doubt.

Becky was born with a spinal disease called spina bifida. She has no feeling in or use of her legs. But although she can only move from the waist up, her disease hasn't slowed her down a bit.

At the age of nine, she began to speak in front of people about her disability. One of her first speaking opportunities was in front of the youth group at her church. The next week, a teenage boy in the youth group who had heard her story approached her and said, "If I was paralyzed, I would be miserable. But seeing you so full of joy—sharing your story and trying to tell others about how good God is while you have to be in a wheelchair the rest of your life—has now changed *my* life."

And that's Becky for you. Her joy is contagious. She is a

girl who has found a faith so life-giving and joy-filling that—in spite of her circumstances—she changes lives all over the world, especially in the country of Romania.

As we were sipping our drinks at Starbucks, Becky informed me that in Romania, when someone has a disability, many times that person is considered cursed, kept indoors, and given no chance at finding purpose in life. That's why Becky goes to Romania every year. She and her parents go with a team to distribute wheelchairs and to tell people with disabilities that God loves them and wants to use them, despite how useless they may have been made to feel. Her love of smiling is changing lives in Romania.

For example, she told me about a Romanian man who approached her mom and asked how her daughter could smile while in a wheelchair. This gave Becky the chance to share the love and hope of Jesus with that man.

Her radiant smile has changed me as well. As I watched her share her story, I was in awe. She admitted to me that the hardest struggle has been loneliness—not many friends, no one she could relate to—especially in middle school and high school. And friends in middle school and high school are *so* important! Can you imagine going so many years without a close girlfriend to share life with? But no matter how many lonely weekends she has spent, how many surgeries she has suffered, or how many times she has longed to walk, Becky has a vibrant faith—a faith that gives her joy, peace, and purpose.

Don't you want that?

My favorite quote from Becky that day at Starbucks was that her "first step will be in heaven with Jesus." *Wow!*

Hebrews 11:1 says, "Now faith is being sure of what we hope for and certain of what we do not see." Becky has that kind of faith. Although she can't see it, she knows that her real body and her real home await her. And they will *far* outweigh any of her trials on this earth.

Jamie Grace

Are you a YouTube fan? If so, next time you are on YouTube, check out a young woman named Jamie Grace.

Jamie Grace uses YouTube as a way to help others and share her faith. She lives with a neurological disease called Tourette's syndrome, or TS. Growing up, Jamie Grace suffered a lot of embarrassing moments because of TS. It causes her to randomly twitch and jolt, stutter, and make uncontrollable sounds (at very untimely moments). But instead of letting TS shame her, she trusted God to claim her—claim her heart and her disease and use them to bring others encouragement. She began to post videos to encourage other teens struggling with this illness. And the response was widespread. So many could relate to her and were grateful to know that they weren't alone in their journeys.

As a creative outlet and escape from the problems that come with her disease, Jamie Grace began to write songs. So on top of posting videos about battling TS, Jamie Grace started posting videos of songs she had written. Most of her songs were love songs to Jesus. Unlike the positive response to the TS videos, the response to her "Jesus" music was spotted with hate messages. Not everyone appreciated her songs

> because of the faith message. She received a lot of hurtful comments and could have easily let herself feel defeated. But just as she refused to let TS weigh her down, she refused to let the judgments of others triumph over her. Instead, because of her willingness to take risks in her walk with God, she kept on posting one song after the other—until a Christian artist named TobyMac discovered her. Now she has signed with a record label and has a hit song on the radio! And it all started with a teenage girl, embarrassed by an incurable disease.

Jamie Grace loved God too much to settle for a shame-filled story. She handed over her heart and asked Him to use her. And look at her now! What an adventure she lives, telling thousands upon thousands how good God is.

Do you want a faith like Jamie Grace? I do! A faith that rises above what the world thinks of me, a faith that boldly tells thousands of people that God loves them, a faith that is so on fire that it inspires songs to fill others with hope and joy.

But the truth is, at times I feel . . .

Bored, Just Bored

I don't always jump up and down about God. If I'm being real (you'll notice throughout this book that "getting real" is one of my favorite things to do), then I'll admit that sometimes I get bored in my faith.

There are times when I can be sitting in church as the preacher gives a message and all I hear is, "Blah, blah, blah." Deep down I'm thinking, *I just want to go eat lunch!*

There are times when the last thing I want to read is the Bible. I'd much rather get on Facebook or pick up the latest *People* magazine.

There are times when I fall asleep in the middle of praying, and when I would rather hang out with friends than with God.

Ever felt that way? Ever just been kind of bored with the whole God thing? If so, then it's your turn to get real. Write about a time when you were feeling blah in your faith. (It could be right now!)

Talk to any one of those girls whom I mentioned earlier, and they will admit that their faith isn't always an adventure. It isn't always on fire. They, too, sometimes feel lukewarm in their journeys with God. We are all going to have ups and downs with God—not because God is up and down, but because we are. And because of that, I need to give you some realistic expectations while reading this book.

What It's Not

First things first. I'm going to tell you what you will *not* get out of this book.

- The goal of this book is *not* to promise you a perfect, vibrant, soaring faith.
- I'm *not* providing you a fix-it-all formula for a faith filled with awe 24/7.
- You will *not* walk away from this book with *all* the answers to having a dynamic faith. I don't have all the answers.
- You will *not* walk away with *all* the ins and outs of what your faith should look like. We are all on unique journeys of faith.

With that being said, you might be wondering, *So . . . what's the point of this book? Looks like you aren't going to offer me any help here.*

What It Is

All right, before you put the book down, let's talk about what I hope you *do* take away from this book.

The goal of this book is to shake you up a little.

No matter where you are in your faith journey—whether you are new to this God thing or you have known what a relationship with Jesus is like your entire life—when you finish this book, I want you to stop settling. Stop settling for a faith that is dull, boring, *blah*. So many of us get stuck in a lifeless faith and just stay there, thinking that this is what life with God is about. No! God wants more for us!

In John 10:10, Jesus says this: "I have come that they may have life, and have it to the full." Do you want a faith that is full of life? I mean soul-feeding, heart-overflowing life? I do! I want *more* in my walk with God. And I think that if you picked up this book, deep down you are yearning for more too.

So to find this full life, we are going to chat about some questions. Questions like, "Why do I get bored with God?" And as we uncover *why*, you and I will have a firmer grip on *how*. *How* can we get *un*bored with God? (Yes, I realize *unbored* isn't an actual word, but in this book it is.)

Stop settling for a faith that is dull, boring, blah.

If you are babysitting a two-year-old who starts throwing a random temper tantrum, you don't know *how* to make him or her feel better until you know *why* in the world that toddler is screaming! And that's why we are going to ask *why*. The more we understand *why* we are stuck in a bored rut, the more we will understand *how* to get out of it.

Finally, toward the end of the book, we will answer the question, "Does God care if I'm bored with Him?" Again, I'm not promising you perfect solutions for a perfect faith. I'm just promising questions to help you search your heart and discussions to guide you into a fuller, richer season of your faith.

Okay, I've rattled on about what my role is in this book and what I hope to offer, but what about you?

You have a *huge* role in this book!

You know what it is? Reading. But not just reading. *Active* reading.

I don't want you to just flip through the pages and read the words but not apply them to your own heart. To *actively* read, I want you to write down your thoughts. And I offer you plenty of chances to do just that. So do it! Active reading also means that you are taking the words and applying them to your own situation. Think through your own life and ask God how the words and ideas in this book can help you right now.

Your role is also to pray. Pray that God will give you a heart that is soft, soft enough for Him to mold and shape you. Soft enough for His words to get through. Soft enough for His revelation to sink in. Only God can take your faith from blah to awe. So to kick off this journey, let's pray together.

> *God, give us soft hearts—hearts that are sensitive to Your voice, hearts that are in a position to be changed. Help us grow in our faith. Help us grow in our understanding of You. May we walk away from this book changed, more in awe of how good You are. Amen.*

2

Behind the Stage, Between the Lines, Beneath the Makeup

Scarily Honest

Okay, I'm about to get pretty honest—scarily honest. I'm about to share some truth that I'm not proud of, give you a sneak peek into the darker corners of my heart that I tend to hide. The truth is, my heart is messy. Really messy. Messier than your room after six of your friends come over for a slumber party. Messier than your hair after spending a summer day at the water park. Messier than the backseat of the family car after an eight-hour road trip. Yep. That messy. Do you think you can handle it? Here it goes . . .

This is the behind-the-stage-between-the-lines-beneath-the-makeup view of Jenna's heart. (As you can see, I never have an issue with wordiness. Umm . . . yeah.)

I can't go through my day without judging someone else. "I can't believe she would wear that!" "Wow, does he really think he can get a girl like her?" Or "I am so glad I'm not like her." Yikes! That brutal honesty can make your stomach hurt.

A lot of times when I do something nice for someone else, I'm doing it just so someone else will think better of me. I want my mom to notice I did the dishes or my neighbor to notice I chased after their dog. I'd also like a pat on my back for going on a mission trip. I'm rarely nice to be nice. Pretty gross confession, right?

There are times when I call other drivers nasty names because I think I'm the only person in the universe who drives correctly. Other times, the last thing I want to do is loan someone money or pay for a friend's meal or lend her my favorite top, because I am stingy with my stuff. I am jealous of others who are smarter and prettier. And at times, it's hard for me to be happy for my friends when they succeed, because deep down I wish that I were the one succeeding. And the list goes on and on . . .

So there it is. My messed-up heart. (And that's just scratching the surface.) Why did I go into all of this? Because I believe it helps us answer our question: Why do we get bored with God?

The answer is our hearts. Our hearts pile up with trash. I shared some of my negative thoughts with you, not to accuse you of having the same issues, but rather to show that we all have major blemishes on our hearts. I don't know what your struggles are. I don't know what's underneath the makeup of your heart. But I bet if we all got honest with ourselves, we would all need more than a touch of powder and lip gloss.

I know this could be a daunting exercise, and it's definitely not a fun one, but it may be helpful to go ahead and look beneath the makeup of your heart. Get real with yourself for a second, and jot down those ugly parts of your heart that are hard to face.

A lot of times when I do something nice for someone else, I'm doing it just so someone else will think better of me.

....

....

....

....

....

The Bible makes it clear that all our hearts have issues. Check out these blunt words:

> **The heart is deceitful above *all* things and beyond cure.**
>
> —Jeremiah 17:9, emphasis mine

> *All* of us also lived . . . at one time, gratifying the cravings of our sinful nature.
>
> —Ephesians 2:3, emphasis mine

> It's what comes out of a person that pollutes: obscenities, lusts, thefts, murders, adulteries, greed, depravity, deceptive dealings, carousing, mean looks, slander, arrogance, foolishness—all these are vomit from the heart. There is the source of your pollution.
>
> —Mark 7:20–23 MSG

I was reading a news article the other day about a study a professor in Switzerland performed on 229 kids. Basically, the study proved how selfish little three- and four-year-olds are. Look at his results:

> In a scenario called the sharing treatment, the child was offered two choices. Choice No. 1: one piece of candy for himself or herself and one piece of candy for another child. Choice No. 2: two pieces for himself or herself, and nothing for the other child.
>
> At age 3 and 4, only 8.7% of children in the sharing treatment chose to give another child they knew one of the pieces of candy. By age 7 and 8, 45% of children chose to share one of the candies.[1]

Thankfully, by age seven or eight, kids start to understand the importance of fairness and sharing. But little kids are selfish! Maybe you babysit or have a little brother or a younger niece. Does anyone have to teach them to be selfish? I don't think so. In fact, what is often one of the first words to come out of little mouths besides *Dada*? It's *mine*!

From the get-go, we have hearts that don't choose God. We choose ourselves. We have selfish, junky hearts by nature.

But maybe you never really knew this. Maybe you have lived your life thinking that you are a "pretty good girl." You haven't sold drugs, shot heroine, or murdered anyone. Your heart can't be *that* bad, right? Wrong. And that's why we get bored with God.

No Need for God

We get bored with God when we do not think we have a need for God.

Why did Jesus come? To save and transform our hearts by giving us undeserved help. When we do not believe our hearts need saving, then we may nibble on Jesus' saving grace instead of devouring it as if our hearts were desperate for it—which they are!

To be grateful for the reality of our hearts *after* Jesus, we have to understand the reality of what our hearts were like *before* Jesus rescued us. And that's why the first part of this chapter asked you to focus on the darkness your heart is capable of. I wanted you to feel icky, in need of a cleanup, in need of Jesus. And Jesus does so much more than just clean up our messy hearts. He gives us entirely new ones!

Check out these verses:

I will give you a new heart and put a new spirit in you.

—Ezekiel 36:26

I have been crucified with Christ and I no longer live, but Christ lives in me.

—Galatians 2:20

So Christ lives in you and gives you a new heart if you put your trust in Him. This is why we aren't discouraged or left hopeless. We have a new, clean heart if we are in Christ!

But that doesn't mean that we instantly start living perfect, God-fearing, God-loving, God-following lives. Earlier, I got real with you about how nasty my heart can sometimes be, even though I put my trust in Jesus and got a new heart years ago. So what's the deal with that?

The best analogy I've read to describe what happens to our hearts when we trust in Jesus comes from a guy named Dwight Edwards. He explains that becoming a Christian is more than a car wash. Sure, God cleans up our gross hearts, but it's so much more than that! Take a look at this:

> It's as if, right there between the power wash and power rinse cycles, a brand new engine was dropped into the car, plus entirely new wiring. Of course the old engine is temporarily left in, and we can choose (foolishly) to operate by it . . . But we don't have to.[2]

So there ya go, girl. You have a brand new engine inside of you (a new heart), but you also still have that clunker engine that gets in the way. The Bible calls this clunker our "flesh"—it's the old sinful self that misleads us and steers us away from God. We will have to battle the flesh for the rest of our lives on this earth. And the flesh is one answer to our "Why do I get bored with God?" question.

How does your flesh get in the way of pursuing an exciting relationship with God?

....

....

....

....

Our flesh will always make us choose ourselves over God. It is selfish. It goes against what God asks us to do, which is to deny ourselves (Luke 9:23). The more we deny our flesh and follow the ways of Jesus, the more our faith will go from *blah* to *awe*.

We get bored with God when we do not think we have a need for God.

Let's pause now and ask God to help us live by our new engines rather than our old ones, so we will desire what *He* wants for us rather than what *we* want.

God, please help us fight the flesh side that turns away from You and makes our faith cold. Instead, help us to live by our new hearts that desire You and desire what is good. Amen.

If you ever question whether it is your flesh or your new heart that is leading you, crack open the Bible. Our new hearts will *always* align with God's Word. In fact, the more you read God's Word, the more you will find yourself operating from the new engine instead of the old clunker. The Bible is like fuel for your new engine. It revs it up, feeds it, and awakens it so that you can make decisions based on God's new heart for you—instead of the old one that will lead you down the wrong path. (Speaking of cracking open the Bible, check out Paul's struggle between his new and old engines in Romans 7:15–25.)

But I Feel Like . . .

Now that we have a better understanding of the status of our hearts, we can break down one more answer to our "Why do I get bored with God?" question: our unreliable feelings. Because we still have our flesh popping up once in a while, we have to be careful of this especially girly side effect of the flesh.

Take a minute to document all the different feelings you have experienced today. Were you frustrated with your mom, angry with a sibling, insecure in the gym, impatient in traffic, appreciative of a friend?

Our feelings can be misleading at times (especially at that time of the month, right, girl?). There are days when I wake up hating the world. I hate my hair. I hate my skin. I hate the chores I have to do around the house. And then, something happens. I have a big glass of ice-cold Coke, I take a nap, I get a text from an old friend, or I eat the juiciest cheeseburger for lunch. And guess what? I feel great! My feelings can be so unreliable!

I know you've heard sayings like, "Follow your heart; it's always right." But we have to be wary of that kind of advice because a lot of our feelings don't come from the new heart God has given us; they come from our flesh. For example, let's check out Katie's story:

Katie

Katie is a junior in high school. She really liked this guy and believed that her "heart" was telling her to "Go for it!" All her friends were pretty skeptical, warning her to stay away. Katie ignored the warnings and decided to "follow her heart," or at least follow her feelings. After Katie had been dating this guy a while, she discovered that he had been cheating on her with another girl during a large part of their relationship. Now Katie is afraid to trust her own feelings. And rightfully so! Our feelings can mislead us.

Even the Bible suggests that we should lean not on ourselves, but on a God whose heart isn't full of up-and-down, crazy emotions. Proverbs 3:5 says, "Trust in the LORD with all your heart and lean not on your own understanding." Instead of letting our feelings rule us, whom does the Bible say to trust? God. Why? Well, let's check out His track record, and I have a hunch you'll see why:

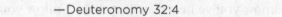

> **He is the Rock, his works are perfect, and all his ways are just. A faithful God who does no wrong, upright and just is he.**
>
> —Deuteronomy 32:4

> **He who is the Glory of Israel does not lie or change his mind; for he is not a man, that he should change his mind.**
>
> —1 Samuel 15:29

> **All your words are true.**
>
> —Psalm 119:160

Circle the words that describe who God is in those verses. Now compare those circled words to what you wrote earlier about all the emotions you have experienced in the last twelve hours. See a difference? God is so consistent, stable, reliable. Our feelings can't always be trusted, but God can.

If we ever *feel* as if God's not that awesome, not doing much except chillin' in heaven . . .

If we ever *feel* as if we cannot hear Him or see Him, and because of that, He probably doesn't care . . .

If we ever *feel* as if our worship songs or prayers are just hitting the ceiling and not reaching heaven . . .

If we ever *feel* as if church isn't that big of a deal, that the Bible is just some made-up story that won't really change any lives . . .

If we ever *feel* bored with God . . .

Why would we trust those feelings? They are *not* reliable!

I have realized that when I'm *feeling* bored with God, this feeling usually comes from my flesh side—the clunker engine. It's just not based on truth. And it isn't because of Him; it's because of me.

Going Deeper

Having up-and-down feelings isn't wrong. Even sometimes having bad feelings toward God isn't wrong. The feeling itself is not the sin or the mistake. It's what we do with the feeling that counts. We can't always control our feelings, but I believe in a God who wants to help us through the emotional roller coaster we girls face. A passage that has helped me stabilize my feelings is Philippians 4:8–9:

> Whatever is true, whatever is noble,
> whatever is right, whatever is pure,
> whatever is lovely, whatever is admirable—
> if anything is excellent or praiseworthy—
> think about such things . . . And the God of
> peace will be with you.

What consumes your mind the most?

....

....

Do you find your thoughts focusing on things that are noble, right, pure, lovely, admirable, excellent, and praiseworthy? When our thoughts are unstable, so are our feelings. Praying Scripture is a great way to ground our feelings in God's truth. Let's pray this verse over our minds and our hearts. It may sound a little like this:

> *God, my thoughts and feelings are all over the place. Please control my thoughts and center them on good, lovely, and admirable things. And please center my feelings on the truth that comes from You. Amen.*

To Sum It Up

Why do we get bored with God?

We don't see the brokenness in our own hearts; therefore, we do not see our need for Jesus. Although we have new hearts through Jesus, our old selves—the "flesh"—still try to mislead us, encouraging us to choose ourselves over God. And finally, this flesh creates feelings that are unreliable. So if we feel bored with God, then that feeling comes from our unreliable flesh, not the truth of who God is.

Knowing this, how do we get unbored with God?

First, we must open our eyes to how messy our hearts are. This creates in us a deep desire and hunger for God, instead of a casual, boring acceptance of Him. We then open our eyes to our new hearts in Jesus. This brings about gratitude and love for what Jesus did to save us. And we pray—we pray that we will live from our "new engines" instead of our old "clunkers."

3

Bored Makes Sense

Sensory Overload

Kim

Kim does her math homework while listening to her favorite band to drown out her brother's tuba practice, while texting her best friend and a guy she likes, while checking periodically to see if someone is on Facebook chat, while her mom is standing in the doorway asking her questions about her weekend plans, while her dad yells at the game that is blaring on the TV down the hall, while she snacks on some gummy bears and daydreams about prom—all at the same time.

Phew! Are you exhausted just by reading that paragraph? Well, probably not, because that may describe your typical day. If you want to play a little game, try counting all the activities going on at the same time in that one little moment of Kim's life. What number did you come up with? I counted ten things (doing homework, listening to music, brother practicing tuba, texting, checking Facebook, mom talking, dad yelling, TV blaring, snacking, and daydreaming). Does that remind you of . . . you?

- The average amount of media for 7th through 12th graders is two and a half hours of TV, one and a half hours of computer, and two and a half hours of music/audio while doing other stuff.
- Forty-five out of one hundred students said the TV is usually on in the house even when it's not being watched.
- Seventy-four percent of 7th through 12th graders have an online profile of some kind.
- The average 7th through 12th grader spends one and a half hours a day sending and receiving texts.[1]

We live in a culture that is on sensory overload! We are constantly *listening* to music, *watching* the latest music video, *tasting* the new frozen yogurt at the joint down the street, *looking* at a new magazine.

What's the primary thing that allows you and me to go hours on end stimulating our senses? Technology. We are plugged into chargers, plugged up with headphones, and tuned in to the show, all while tuning out Mom.

Spend a minute documenting your technology time on an average day. How many hours and minutes do you spend using different types of technology (iPod, TV, radio/Pandora, Internet, etc.)?

We live in a world that appeals to our senses. I just watched twenty minutes of television, focusing on the commercials to prove this point. Check out what I found.

The first thing I noticed is that our country is obsessed with food! Sheesh! Second thing I noticed: almost every commercial I watched appealed to my senses. I wanted to *look* at myself in the mirror after I saw the beach body dieting commercial. I wanted to *taste* a snack after I watched the cheesy crackers commercial. I wanted to *touch* the softness of the couches on sale at the furniture warehouse (and take a nap). It's no accident that these commercials are stimulating our senses.

I was reading a book the other day called *Brand Sense: Sensory Secrets Behind the Stuff We Buy*. The author shared a story about his friend shopping for a birthday present in the middle of winter, yet she walked into a store that sells beachwear all year long thinking she would just look at the jewelry. But soon she found herself browsing the swimsuit racks. She thought it strange that she all of a sudden wanted to buy a swimsuit in the middle of winter, until she noticed something—a smell. It smelled like summer. She asked the store clerk if she was going crazy, but sure enough, the "clerk led her to a corner of the store and pointed to a machine that was pumping out a subtle but discernible smell of coconuts. (In the end, she didn't buy the swimsuit, but a week later she booked a trip to Fiji.)"[2]

Isn't that crazy? But I have an even crazier factoid for you. This quote actually made me sad: "I hate to disappoint you, but there's no such thing as a new car smell—at least an organic one. It, the 'New Car' fragrance, can be found packed in aerosol-filled canisters on the factory floor."[3]

There's no "new car" smell? That's one of my favorite smells in the world! (I still don't want to believe it.)

The world we experience with God is even more real than the world we experience with our senses.

But back to the point. We live in a world that is throwing advertising darts straight at our senses, a world where technology is king. Am I trying to tell you that stimulating our senses is bad? No! That's how we live! God gave us our senses. They give us enjoyment and alert us to danger. They help us connect to other people, and they ultimately point us to God.

When we see a sunset, may we remember the true Son. When we listen to a melody, may we remember that He sings over us (Zephaniah 3:17). When we run our fingers through our hair, may we remember He knows the number of hairs on our heads (Matthew 10:30). Senses are good things, designed by God and pointing us to God.

But let's get real. Most of the time, this sensory-driven world we live in blinds us to God. It keeps us too focused on *this* reality—a reality we can see with our eyes and hear with our ears. And that's when senses become dangerous, because the world we experience with God is even more real than the world we experience with our senses. God is all about another reality—a realm that we can call the *supernatural*.

Is the Supernatural Super-Weird?

Could sensory overload be part of the answer to our "Why am I bored with God?" question? Let's think about it.

There may be quite a few of us who have tried to hang out with God, but after sitting a while and not *hearing* anything . . . after praying a while and not *seeing* results . . . after reading the Bible and not *feeling* His touch, are we thinking, *Where is this God anyway? And what is the big deal? I don't feel any different. I'd rather hang out with a friend I can actually see, hear, touch, and... well... smell!* See, it makes *sense* that we can get bored with God.

The life this world promotes can clash with what God is all about.

The presence of God is beyond our ordinary senses of smelling, touching, hearing, and seeing. He is supernatural. And the world, at times, masks the supernatural by bombarding our natural senses. In fact, the idea of the supernatural could kind of weird you out. If it does, then that's proof—proof that you are a victim of the world. But Jesus wants us to shake off this mentality because it makes for a boring faith. Check out Jesus' prayer for His followers:

They are not of the world any more than I am of the world. My prayer is not that you take them out of the world but that you protect them from the evil one.

—John 17:14–15

Read that verse again, but this time cross out the words "they" or "them" and replace them with your own name. What does this verse say about you?

....

....

....

....

We live in two worlds—or better, in one world with two parts, one part that we can see and one part that we cannot. We are urged . . . to act as though the unseen world . . . is, in fact, more weighty and more real . . . than the part of reality we can see.

—John Eldredge, *Waking the Dead*[4]

You Are Not an Alien . . . Well . . . Kind Of

If you are a Christian, you are no longer of this world. We aren't talking extraterrestrial here. You aren't able to peel back your skin to reveal some kind of E.T.-looking creature underneath. That's just weird. But the Bible does call us *aliens*, meaning "strangers" to this world, because our real home is heaven. Our real lives are found outside of this world, in another realm. So I guess, in a way, we *are* aliens.

> **There are no ordinary people. Everyone I have come in contact with is an eternal being.**
>
> **—C. S. Lewis, *The Weight of Glory*[5]**

What if that's what you kept in mind as you walked the halls of your school? Every person you pass is eternal. They are on their way to either an eternity in heaven or an eternity in hell. I bet that would change the way you saw the football players, the quiet math genius, or the class clown. How would that change the way you see others? And yourself?

....

....

....

....

....

....

Now that is thinking supernaturally! Looking at people, knowing that they are more than walking bodies—they are walking souls! It makes this life so much more exciting when we think that way. It makes our relationships with God more exciting too.

We will not get unbored with God until we start making the supernatural a part of our physical lives so that the mundane becomes mystical. Too bad that's not always the case. We forget about the supernatural, forget about a God who is actively moving beyond what we can see, hear, smell, or touch.

And there is one guy whose biggest job is to make sure we don't see or believe in the supernatural realm of God. He loves it when we grow blah in our faith, limiting God to our physical senses. But he hates being talked about—which is why we are about to do it, of course.

The Enemy

Okay, I realize this is a book for girls, and talking about war and battle stuff is somewhat masculine, but do whatever you have to do to soak this truth in. (If that means imagining yourself wearing armor that is girly pink with diamonds, be my guest.) Go ahead, release your inner warrior princess!

The truth is this: within this supernatural world, God has an enemy. Glance back at John 17:14–15, which you read earlier. From whom does Jesus ask God to protect you?

....

....

That's right. The "evil one." The Enemy, also known as Satan. He is out to "steal and kill and destroy" anything that would bring us joy and love and life from God (John 10:10 NCV). He is constantly at war with God, shooting arrows of flaming lies at God's children (Ephesians 6:16). That means you, girl! These lies can be anything and everything that goes against God's truth: "You aren't worth it." "You aren't beautiful." "You can't do anything right." Even this boredom problem we have with God stems from lies the Enemy has thrown at us: "God doesn't exist." "God doesn't care about you, so why care about Him?" "Why read the Bible? It's boring! Just turn on the TV." These are all lies, and maybe you have heard them. I know I have.

The Enemy wants us to be so tied up and trapped in the junk of this world that we cannot see the spiritual world, we cannot see how alive and awesome our God is. The Enemy doesn't even want us to see him. "Why?" you ask.

C. S. Lewis wrote a book called *The Screwtape Letters*, which is written from the voice of a demon named Screwtape. Screwtape says, "When they believe in us, we cannot make them materialists and skeptics."[6] The Enemy wants you to forget all about him! If you don't know he's there, you won't fight him. He wants you to become materialistic and skeptical of God so that you will be totally oblivious to the war that is being fought for your heart.

A war? For your heart? That's right!

The Enemy is battling for your heart. But the great news is that you have a God who is also warring for your heart, your affection, and a relationship with you. He is a mighty warrior who cares for you (Exodus 15:3). Did you read that? God is doing bloody battle against the Enemy for *you*! God is fighting the Enemy who wants to turn your heart away from God and weaken your faith. It is happening every second of every day—and most of the time, we don't even know the war is taking place! We are sleeping through the battle.

Sleeping Through the Battle

Are you a deep sleeper? Ever slept through an alarm, a movie, or even a class in school? Maybe you are always the first to fall asleep at a slumber party while everyone else is dancing, eating, laughing, and eventually spraying whipped cream all over your sleeping bag since you were the first to doze off. No matter how deep a sleeper you are, I bet you couldn't sleep if bombs were exploding, swords were clanging, and bullets were whizzing by your bed. (If you could, we have a problem.) Yet we do this all the time! We are napping while a vicious battle for our souls is warring all around us!

No wonder we have sleepy, dull faiths! We are snoozing while Satan tries to defeat us, to steal any joy we could find in a faith in God.

Girl, it's time to suit up and fight for the exhilarating faith God wants for you to have. Wake up! Shake up your boring faith!

So how do we wake up and fight? Check out this verse:

Put on the full armor of God so that you can take your stand against the devil's schemes. For our struggle is not against flesh and blood, but against the rulers, against the authorities, against the powers of this dark world and against the spiritual forces of evil in the heavenly realms.

—Ephesians 6:11–12

Want to know what God's armor looks like? Suit up with this list from Ephesians 6!

- Truth is your belt.
- Righteousness is your breastplate.
- The gospel of peace is fitted around your feet.
- Faith is your shield.
- Salvation is your helmet.
- And the Word of God is your sword.

What is the best way to fight evil? Know the Word of God. It is your sword and the belt that secures you. Choose to live like Jesus. This righteousness will guard your heart. Ask God for more faith. This faith will protect you from doubt. And trust in your salvation. This will fight insecurity. At the end of these verses in Ephesians, Paul tells us to pray, pray, pray. Prayer is the most powerful weapon for you to use in the fight against the Enemy.

Battles Ain't Boring!

I don't know about you, but I think a battle ain't boring. It's full of suspense, drama, tears, and emotion. When we ask God to open our hearts beyond our senses and allow us to enter the reality of the supernatural, you and I get to take part in this exciting battle. Don't worry, you aren't going to have to wear sweaty armor and pick up a sword, but you will experience just how *real* the spiritual realm is. And experiencing the spiritual realm can bring life to a dull faith like nothing else!

Sarah

When Sarah was twenty years old, she join a missionary program called YWAM (You With A Mission). Through YWAM, Sarah joined a team of people who traveled to Cambodia to share the message of Jesus. Little did she know that her faith was about to brush up against the supernatural in a way that would forever change her.

Sarah had always believed in the supernatural miracles of the Bible. But she questioned if God could work miracles today. That is, until she met Wade.

Sarah met Wade at a home for people with disabilities. He was thirteen years old and was unable to stand for more than three seconds before his legs began to quiver. He suffered from a disease called Bone Tuberculosis. But what he lacked in muscle strength, he made up for with a lively personality and bright smile that warmed Sarah's heart. She sat with Wade, played with him, and at the end of the day, she and her friends prayed for healing as they laid hands on his stiff body. Sarah remembers thinking, *I just need the faith of a mustard seed, and this boy will be healed.* No visible miracle happened during the prayer, so when they said good-bye, they left unaware that God was already stirring.

The next day, Sarah bumped into an American man who had been volunteering at the home where Wade lived. His eyes lit up when he saw Sarah, breathlessly exclaiming, "You won't believe this, but since we prayed for Wade, he has been running, walking, even riding a bike!" Sarah was overwhelmed with joy. She told me in a message, "My faith in God has increased 100 percent. God loves to show His power! It was truly a modern-day miracle, with God using a very simple girl who had the faith of a mustard seed."

The supernatural woke up Sarah's faith. She saw a side of God that floored her, wowed her. God had used her to heal Wade, and now she hungers to see the powerful work of God more and more in her life.

We do not hunger for God because we have not asked God to help us see beyond the physical. We have not asked Him to show us his supernatural power. So start asking! Ask God to show you more of Himself in math class, around the kitchen table, as you lie in bed.

Sarah tasted the reality of God and the reality of another realm—His healing power had flowed through her and into Wade. Sarah had awakened to the battle warring for Wade's heart. And this stirred her own heart. It made her want to fight more, search for God more, and look beyond the physical.

So why do we find ourselves bored with God? Well, the Enemy wants to blind us from seeing the supernatural, from fully experiencing God. Satan knows that when we do experience the supernatural, we will never be the same—kind of like Sarah.

Going Deeper

Have you ever had a Meg moment—a time when you could sense the supernatural? If so, explain. If not, why do you think you haven't?

To sense God in our everyday lives, we have to get to know the Holy Spirit. The words *Holy Spirit* may make you uncomfortable or just confuse you. But He is very real, and until you understand more about Him and how He works in your life, you will never get out of the bored slump. So let's talk about Him a little bit.

If you choose to believe and follow Jesus, you have the Spirit in you. Jesus said, "I will ask the Father, and he will give you another Counselor to be with you forever" (John 14:16).

"In this case," writes Francis Chan, "the Greek word *another* means another that is just like the first."[7] That means the Holy Spirit is Jesus. Jesus is the Spirit. You have the Creator of the universe in you!

The Spirit is who gives you eyes to see God, ears to hear God, and a heart that can be touched by God. Read the following verses and find out some of what the Holy Spirit can do *through* and *in* you. And then write down how these verses might shake up your boring faith life.

The Spirit encourages and strengthens you. "Then the church throughout Judea, Galilee and Samaria enjoyed a time of peace. It was strengthened; and encouraged by the Holy Spirit, it grew in numbers, living in the fear of the Lord" (Acts 9:31).

The Spirit convicts you. "When he comes, he will convict the world of guilt" (John 16:8).

The Spirit guides you. "Those who are led by the Spirit of God are sons of God" (Romans 8:14).

The Spirit blesses you. "But the fruit of the Spirit is love, joy, peace, patience, kindness, goodness, faithfulness, gentleness and self-control" (Galatians 5:22–23).

Can you believe all this? You have deity power in you, girl! That means through Him, *anything* in your life is possible! It is through the spirit of Jesus in you that you experience the supernatural in your daily life. And get ready. He will shake you up!

When was the last time you felt the Holy Spirit leading you to do something and you obeyed him?

It's easy to quench the Spirit in our lives. Just as you begin to forget the sound of a friend's voice after she moves away, we can create distance with God, and His voice (the Spirit) is distant. When we are living lives that don't look like Jesus' life, when we are too caught up in the sensory world, this can quench the Spirit and, in turn, quench our faith.

Do you think you have a life that is led by the Holy Spirit? If not, what (or who) in your life is keeping the Spirit from being louder? And what can you do to sense God and the supernatural more in your life?

To be Spirit-led means that we are Jesus-led. We live lives that honor Him. We spend time with Him—talking to Him, reading His Word. When we hear His voice, we step out and follow it, even if we end up being wrong. Living by the Spirit takes practice and time, and the more we do it, the more we will see the supernatural unveiled right in front of us. It's been there all along. Now it's time to experience it.

Let's close in prayer.

God, I pray that You will give me eyes to see You and ears to hear You. I pray that You will take away anything that blocks my heart from experiencing how real You are. I love You. Amen.

To Sum It Up

Why do we get bored with God?

We live in a world that is all about our physical senses, blinding us to the world beyond what we see, hear, taste, touch, and smell. We have an Enemy who blinds us from seeing how awesome our warrior God is and who keeps us spiritually asleep so that we do not stand up and fight for the exciting faith God wants for us.

Knowing this, how do we get unbored with God?

We ask God to help us see beyond the physical. We fight, using the spiritual weapons talked about in Ephesians 6. And we spend time with God in the Bible and through prayer, asking Him to remove anything that is keeping us from seeing Him.

4

Made-in-China God

Styling Me

I wouldn't say I tortured her. Maybe slightly afflicted. But torture would be too harsh a word. Sara, my little sister, was always an experiment, *my* experiment. And when I say experiment, I don't mean that I duct-taped her to the hood of our Barbie Power Wheels and off-roaded through the woods. (Don't get any ideas.)

No, Sara was more like my model, my muse, my doll. I loved dressing Sara up, styling her hair, painting makeup on her face. Of course, I was my own model too.

I stumbled across some pretty embarrassing home videos of my friends and me when we were younger. We used to cake on our moms' makeup and dress up for our latest "music video," "swimsuit shoot" (please tell me I'm not the *only* one who ever did this!), or "runway show." A lot of girls—like me, and possibly you—have braided their dolls' hair, dressed up their Barbies (or their little sisters), and attacked their faces with bright red lipstick and turquoise eye shadow.

Oh, the lengths we girls will go to and the money we will spend to style ourselves. Want to know how much women spend on beauty?

Even though our country has seen an economic downturn in recent years, American women spend some $7 billion a year on cosmetics alone![1] And that doesn't include other things like trips to the salon, manicures, or pedicures.

Now, if you are more of a tomboy, first of all, I'm jealous because you don't have any of those embarrassing home videos like I do. And second of all, I promise I'm about to relate to you.

That word *style* goes beyond music videos, makeovers, and dolls. We have a desire to *style* life. We *fashion* our futures. We *design* our destinies. We *remodel* our reputations and *create* our careers. Just as I used to make over my face for the camera to feel glamorous, I had dreams of a picture-perfect, glamorous life. I used to mentally style what my perfect husband was going to look like, along with all the details of my dream home. (It was a picket-fenced, white-painted, red-shuttered house with a wide, wraparound porch. In case you wanted to know. Oh! And don't forget the big oak tree with the tire swing. Okay. I'll stop.) See? I tend to design the life I can't see yet.

Long before prom night came, I dreamed of exactly how it would unfold. All through my senior year of high school, I daydreamed about how I would walk across the stage at graduation in the perfect heels. I guess, in my mind, I've always had a life list of what I wanted to do, what was going to happen, how everything would be. Do you ever do that? Style your life?

What in your future, about yourself, or even about tomorrow have you already styled in your mind—your reputation, your dream boyfriend, college? Do you ever give yourself an "Extreme Life Makeover" in your head?

Styling God

You know what else I style? God.

Sometimes I find myself dressing Him up to be whatever god I need Him to be at that time. I tend to create what God looks like, how He acts, what He is doing . . . all in my own little head.

Superhero God

When I was little, I pictured God to be much like the picture of Jesus I colored in my Sunday school coloring books. He had blue eyes, of course, dark hair, and a white smile. We used to sing a song in Sunday school that went a little bit like this: "My God is so big, so strong and so mighty. There's nothing my God cannot do!" *Clap. Clap.* (The claps were my favorite part.) And because of that song, I believed there was nothing God couldn't do! He had big muscles and could swoop in at any moment and save me from my problems. I believed that He heard me pray and took care of me. My very own superhero! It was awesome! But that only lasted so long. Because then middle school hit.

Sidekick God

In middle school God was less of a superhero and more of my sidekick. The show was less about God and more about me. He went from being the star to the understudy, the pilot to the copilot. Life in middle school was all about *my* problems, *my* friends, *my* popularity status, *my* outfits. And when I could fit God into the "Jenna Show," He was always faithful. But because my life revolved around me, God started losing His star power in my life. He wasn't *that* big of a deal. Sure, He loved me, but so what? So did my parents and my sisters. You know what *was* a big deal? My crush, crushing back on me. Now *that* was cool! I guess, in my mind, God was Robin and I was Batman. I could run my life, and if I ever wanted Him around, I would ask Him to show up. And then high school hit.

Cereal Box God

In high school my world got bigger. And with a bigger life came more options. More friend options, more weekend activity options, even more faith options.

Think about it this way: Have you ever stopped to count the number of different cereals in your local grocery store? If not, you should. That's your homework for today. Believe it or not, I took the time to count the cereal boxes at my grocery store. I know it's pretty lame that I actually did that, but you might be surprised to hear that more than three hundred varieties of cereal line the shelves at my local grocery store. *Three hundred!* Do we have options or what?

I tend to create what God looks like, how He acts, what He is doing . . . all in my own little head.

Okay, here's the point I want to make after looking like a weirdo at the grocery store: God became another option to me in high school. He was something I could choose to acknowledge one day and choose to doubt the next. He might have been a strong option during the times I spent at church camp or at a fun Christian retreat. I would come back all excited about faith. But then what happened? A few days later another option took first place. With so many different people, places, and things to do, I found myself looking at God as if He were a box of cereal. "Hmm . . . maybe I'll spend time with God today, but then again, there's always my friend's tournament, and then there's that birthday party for Steven, and my favorite show is about to come on. I don't know. God, I think You get the boot today. Sorry."

If you get honest with yourself right now, who is God to you these days? Is He your best friend, a stranger, or is He nonexistent? Maybe He's some genie-in-a-bottle that you talk to only when you *really* need a prayer to be answered. Maybe He is just some old wizard with a long white beard, keeping an eye on you while reclining on a couch of clouds. Maybe He is the dad you never had. Maybe he is a judgmental, finger-in-your-face guy, picking at your flaws. Who is God to you? How have you styled Him in your mind?

Limiting God

I have spent a lifetime limiting God to fit what I had in mind. But I don't believe it's just me. We live in a consumer society. What we want is what we get. So instead of letting God be God, instead of resting in the fact that He is unfathomable, unimaginable, I have custom-made Him to fit my life. I have made Him fathomable, imaginable. Instead of asking Him to show me who He is, I tell Him who He is.

Do you want to know the primary reason that I, personally, have struggled with spiritual boredom? Because I have been worshiping a god I created, one I styled to be who I needed him to be. A god I can control? That's not God at all!

I had expectations of who He should be. I expected Him to answer my prayers in my way. I expected Him to make life easy for me. I expected Him to help me feel His presence all the time. I expected Him to prevent all my family members and friends from dying, give me A's on all my tests, and hang a green arrow in the clouds pointing to the college I should go to and the job I should take. I was believing in a god that I created. And when we do that, then *of course* we will be bored with God!

Who wants to worship a god based on our limited, pee-wee, human brains? But that's exactly what I was doing. I created my own personal "made-in-Jenna" god.

So here we see another answer to our "Why do I get bored with God?" question.

We get bored with God when we rely on our own conceptions. But we get blown away by God when we rely on His revelation.

A. W. Tozer once said, "What comes to our minds when we think about God is the most important thing about us."[2] *Why* is it the most important thing about us? Well, because if the first images of God that come to our mind derive from our own conclusions and not real truth, then we aren't worshiping the true God.

I believe God wants us to know that if we are bored with Him, we aren't bored with the true God; we are bored with an idea of God—an idea others have created, religion has created, our own minds have created. We get bored with God when we rely on our own conceptions. But we get blown away by God when we rely on His revelation.

Let's stop a minute and just ask God to help us out with this style problem we have. Do you feel as though you have created a smaller god in your head? How might you be limiting Him?

....

....

....

....

....

Going Deeper

When God came to earth, He was not at all what people expected. Jesus did not fit the majestic mold everyone had created.

What? No crown?

What? No wealth?

What? No fame?

What? No flames blazing out of His mouth or lightning bolts shooting from His toes?

Nope. Nope. Nope. And again, nope.

Instead, read the following verses to see the type of man Jesus was:

This will be a sign to you: You will find a baby wrapped in cloths and lying in a manger.

—Luke 2:12

He grew up before him like a tender shoot, and like a root out of dry ground. He had no beauty or majesty to attract us to him, nothing in his appearance that we should desire him. He was despised and rejected by men, a man of sorrows, and familiar with suffering.

—Isaiah 53:2-3

While Jesus was having dinner at Matthew's house, many tax collectors and "sinners" came and ate with him and his disciples.

—Matthew 9:10

Jesus—God in the flesh—was born in a stable for animals, came from a poor carpenter's family, was plain looking, was despised by many, and hung out with all the outsiders—tax collectors, prostitutes, and other "sinners."

Do you believe that people thought this was how God was going to be when He came to earth? How do you think Jesus went against the people's own creations (or "styles") of God?

....

....

....

....

....

From the beginning, God has surprised His people with His compassion, His words, His miracles, His humility. He is not a God to be styled or fashioned by man. Nope. *He* styled and fashioned *us*.

Check out these verses about the people who were amazed and surprised by Jesus. Circle the people's reactions to Jesus.

> The men were amazed and asked, "What kind of man is this? Even the winds and the waves obey him!"
>
> —Matthew 8:27

> And when the demon was driven out, the man who had been mute spoke. The crowd was amazed and said, "Nothing like this has ever been seen in Israel."
>
> —Matthew 9:33

> Coming to his hometown, he began teaching the people in their synagogue, and they were amazed. "Where did this man get this wisdom and these miraculous powers?" they asked.
>
> —Matthew 13:54

We *have* to spend time in His Word to get to know what God's heart is like. Once we do, we will find ourselves just as amazed in our faith as the people you just read about. I'll get you kick-started by sharing one of my favorite paragraphs that describes our Creator. These verses talk about how out-of-the-box, mind-blowing, and breathtaking God truly is. Breathe in these words and ask God to help them sink into your heart.

> Oh, the depth of the riches of the wisdom and knowledge
> of God!
> How unsearchable his judgments,
> and his paths beyond tracing out!
> "Who has known the mind of the Lord?
> Or who has been his counselor?"
> "Who has ever given to God,
> that God should repay him?"
> For from him and through him and to him are all things.
> To him be the glory forever! Amen.
>
> —Romans 11:33–36

Let's close out by talking with God about our styling problem.

> *God, I want to know who You really are. I want to believe in the one true God. A God who parted the Red Sea, healed the sick with a single touch, and raised the dead with a simple word. Forgive me for trying to limit Your limitlessness. Give me a deeper understanding and fresh admiration for You. Amen.*

To Sum It Up

Why do we get bored with God?

We tend to worship a God we have created with our finite minds. When we worship a limited god, our faith is limited.

Knowing this, how do we get unbored with God?

First we must become aware of how we see or understand God to be, and then we must align our perception with the Bible. To truly understand who God is, we have got to crack open that Bible daily! And we can always pray that God opens our hearts to how unfathomable He is. He can give us some pretty life-changing glimpses.

5

Comfy, Cozy, Curled Up

Too Real

In the middle of the twentieth century, Richard Wurmbrand spent fourteen years in prison because of his faith in Jesus Christ. He began an underground church in Romania, a church that met in basements, in the woods, and in other secret places. It was a time when Communism was in power and Christians were persecuted. In his book, *Tortured for Christ*, Wurmbrand recounts the horrific scenes he witnessed and personally experienced in a prison. Fingernails pulled out, prison cells full of starving rats *and* people, beatings, hours upon hours standing in a box lined with spikes that would pierce the skin anytime a muscle flinched.[1]

I put the book down after reading a few chapters and immediately turned on the television. I didn't want to think about it. I fought God's voice, nudging me to go *there*–a place that really existed, a place where evil laughed in the face of good, a place where innocence was stripped from young girls and dignity was stripped from men, a place that didn't make sense in my world of comfort and freedom. It was just *too real*!

I wanted to plug myself up with headphones, go to the mall, call a friend . . . anything but mentally go to that dark place and feel the terrors these tortured Christians faced. I wanted to run away from God's voice. I don't know if you have ever tried outrunning God's voice, but it's kind of difficult—more than difficult; it's impossible. (Just ask Jonah!) It didn't matter how loud I cranked the volume on the television, God's voice was louder. So I gave in. I finally listened. I went *there*.

It took me a while. But I picked the book back up and continued to read the stories, the stories of old days and of present times—people all around the world marginalized, beaten, and dying for their faith in Jesus. "There are more Christian martyrs today than there were in AD 100—in the days of the Roman Empire," when Christians were thrown into the coliseum and eaten by lions.[2] Knowing that this kind of persecution is happening today broke me. I cried. Then I talked to God:

> *God, I don't get it! These people gave up their lives for You. You were everything to them. And here I am with a lifeless faith. They have something I don't.*

One story in particular stood out among all the others. I want to share it with you on one condition: that you will *go there.* Don't turn on the television like I did. Just think about the persecuted and pray. Pray for the people all over the world who at *this* moment are suffering for a hope that evil hates. This is a reality right *now.* Christians in India, China, Turkey, North Korea—the list goes on—are sacrificing comfort, family, wealth, freedom, and even their own lives for what they believe.

A Prisoner Dressed in White

"One of our workers in the Underground church was a young girl. The Communist police discovered that she secretly spread Gospels and taught children about Christ. They decided to arrest her. But to make the arrest as agonizing and painful as they could, they decided to delay her arrest a few weeks, until the day she was to be married. On her wedding day, the girl was dressed as a bride—the most wonderful, joyous day in a girl's life! Suddenly, the door burst open and the secret police rushed in.

"When the bride saw the secret police, she held out her arms toward them to be handcuffed. They roughly put the manacles on her wrists. She looked toward her beloved, then kissed the chains and said, 'I thank my heavenly Bridegroom for this jewel He has presented to me on my marriage day. I thank Him that I am worthy to suffer for Him.' She was dragged off, with weeping Christians and a weeping bridegroom left behind. They knew what happens to young Christian girls in the hands of Communist guards."

The bride didn't see her groom until five years later. Five years. Think about that. How old were you five years ago? So much time. So much pain. But her groom waited on her. She returned looking like an old woman, broken and abused, yet she said something that made me rethink my comfortable, cushiony, Christian world:

"It was the least I could do for Christ."[3]

Okay, are you like me right now?

"The least I could do!" *What?!* She just spent five years in prison! Arrested on her wedding day—the day every little girl dreams about. Five years at the mercy of men who raped her, beat her, mocked her. And she said it was the least she could do? Am I missing something here? How could she willingly suffer for Jesus? What was it about her faith that made her praise God while being handcuffed to darkness? What did she have in her relationship with God that I don't have?

"It was the least I could do for Christ."

Passion.

The passion of Christianity is that I deliberately sign away my own rights and become a bond-slave of Jesus Christ.

—Oswald Chambers, *My Utmost for His Highest*[4]

When someone is passionate about Jesus, her life is consumed by Him. She thinks about Jesus, talks about Jesus, lives like Jesus. And to most of the world, this looks pretty weird. Why? Because Jesus didn't live like the rest of the world lived.

This young bride had encountered a love from God that radically invaded every ounce of who she was. And this love stirred within her a deep passion that changed her. Her life reflected this passion, and that's why the Communist police easily spotted her. Her life looked different than everyone else's. She was the opposite of bored. She wasn't humdrum in her faith. She was consumed with a fire for God that no prison cell could extinguish.

Being Bored Is . . . Cool?

What is the opposite of boredom? Well, to prevent you from thinking too hard, I'll tell you. I looked up the dictionary antonym for boredom, and here are a couple of opposites: *excitement* and *pleasure*. Passion—like that of the young bride—would also stand on the opposing side of boredom. To have pleasure, excitement, or passion for God does not always bring us the approval of the world. And I think that's yet another answer to our "Why am I bored with God?" question.

Some of us are bored with God because it's easy. It's accepted by the world. It's accepted by us. Really. Think about it.

Who are the cool kids at your school? Are any of them passionate about Jesus? So passionate that their lives look like His? Or are they the ones who wave off God, blow off faith, and live it up however they want?

I don't know. Maybe loving God is cool at your school. If so, that's great. But in general, if we look at what the world promotes when we turn on the TV or read a magazine, what are the trends? Who are the popular faces? The world doesn't necessarily put Christians on a pedestal. And the world definitely doesn't advertise the Christian lifestyle as "exciting" or "pleasurable."

So why do we get bored with God? Well, could it be that we subconsciously remain apathetic toward this God thing because passion for God might mean rejection by our peers?

Passion ≠ Popularity

I have a friend who moved to America about three years ago from Vietnam. She decided to bravely leave everything familiar and friendly to be foreign and flustered. So she packed up her things, and she left for New York at the age of fifteen.

Coming from a Buddhist background, my friend had no intention of exploring Christianity, but thankfully God doesn't work within our intentions. He put Christian after Christian in her path until she finally told me one afternoon in her broken English, "I think I learn to be Christian."

Excited about this new faith, she cherished the Bible I gave her and couldn't wait to read it. Her heart looked like a hot air balloon, fired up by God and soaring high into the sky. But it didn't take long for that balloon to rip and sink a little lower. See, my friend, so thrilled about this new love for God, began to share her faith with her sister, expecting enthusiasm in return. Unfortunately, she met resistance. Converting to Christianity "dishonors" a Buddhist family. It's not accepted. My friend is slowly learning that a loud, exciting faith in God is an adventurous path, but not the easiest path. And it can run into rejection. To this day, she still has not been able to tell her parents of her newfound faith for fear of being completely cut off from her family.

We are never promised that passion for God brings popularity. Actually, we are warned of just the opposite:

> In fact, everyone who wants to live a godly life in Christ Jesus will be persecuted.
>
> —2 Timothy 3:12

Left Out

Emily

After growing up in Texas her entire life, at age fourteen Emily had to leave her closest friends and the only home she had ever known. She didn't just move to a different city. No. Try different country. She and her family moved to Germany, where life looked very different from her old life in the hill country of conservative Texas. In Germany, most of her classmates went out to the clubs, drank, and smoked. She was one of the only Christians at her school, so she felt pretty alone on the weekends. After she finally made a close friend, it wasn't long before her friend stopped hanging out with her and began to hang out with the popular party group. "So then I started to think maybe I just wasn't cool enough, because every time I was asked to go out partying I said no," she told me in a Facebook message. Emily knows what it's like to feel on the outside as a Christian.

Moses

It must have been a lonely job for Moses. There he was, appointed by God to deliver the Israelites after some four hundred or more years in slavery to Egypt. At the end of chapter 4 in Exodus, the Israelite elders were praising God for sending Moses to deliver them from the Egyptians. So marching up to Pharaoh (head honcho over Egypt), giving him a piece of his mind, Moses and his brother Aaron said, "This is what the LORD, the God of Israel, says: 'Let my people go'" (Exodus 5:1). But it wasn't that easy. Pharaoh didn't let them go . . . for a long time.

It only took a chapter for Moses and Aaron to go from the cool guys to the loser guys. At the end of chapter 5, we read of the Israelites' anger toward ole Mo: "May the LORD look upon you and judge you! You have made us a stench to Pharaoh" (Exodus 5:21). You see, Moses had demanded that Pharaoh release the Israelites, but instead Pharaoh defiantly gave the Israelite slaves a heavier load.

Moses, just get ready, buddy. Those harsh words from the Israelites foreshadow a long history of rejection and frustration. Once Moses rescued the Israelites from Egyptian slavery, he still had to put up with those grumpy people for forty years! And we aren't just talking about a small group that he was in charge of. Scholars estimate that the number of Israelites was in the millions! Over 600,000 males alone. Tag on women and children, and what do you have? A massive movement of moody people![5] Over and over again, Moses was badgered and rejected. Here is one of many examples:

> But the people were thirsty for water there, and they grumbled against Moses. They said, "Why did you bring us up out of Egypt to make us and our children and livestock die of thirst?"
>
> Then Moses cried out to the LORD, "What am I to do with these people? They are almost ready to stone me." (Exodus 17:3–4)

It would have been so easy to give up. But Moses didn't give up; he put up—putting up with those doubters time and time again. Why? He had a faith that was bigger than his fear of rejection. He had seen God's power, heard God's voice, and experienced God's deliverance out of Egypt. He knew living for God was the only way to freedom, even when everyone else told him he was crazy. Had he listened to the crowd, they would have all still been stuck in Egypt!

See? A passionate faith doesn't always bring more friends. If anything, a lot of people may not understand you and may even exclude you.

Okay, so we looked at an Old Testament bigwig. Now let's look at a New Testament hero. Meet Paul.

Paul

This guy started out as a Christian hater. He called himself a Hebrew of Hebrews and a zealous Pharisee (Philippians

3:4–6). Translation: he knew the Old Testament law inside and out, held a position of religious power, and persecuted anyone who meddled with his Jewish beliefs. All that to say, you can only *imagine* what his family, friends, and community thought, said, and did once he decided to become the man he lived to persecute! And Paul didn't just become a Christian. He lived and died in the name of Jesus. That means that Paul lost *all* that was comfortable, *all* that he loved for this new Christianity thing. Talk about a passionate faith! And although we don't have his parents or friends on record telling him how crazy he was, we know from Scripture that Paul encountered deep persecution when he gave all he had for Christ:

> "You are out of your mind, Paul!" he shouted. "Your great learning is driving you insane."
>
> —Acts 26:24

> "What is this babbler [Paul] trying to say?"
>
> —Acts 17:18

Paul was beaten, thrown into prison, and stoned for his faith. But no matter what, Paul held fast to God. Why? Because he had been transformed by the love of Jesus—a love he had never experienced through anything else. And he chose to live for this love instead of the love of the world.

Can you, like Moses and Paul, say that you live for God's love more than the world's love? Or do you live to be loved and accepted by the world?

Comfy, Cozy, Curled-Up Faith

Paul was thrown *out*, knocked *out*, and locked *out* so many times that I don't know how he ever felt "in" as a Christian. And isn't that what most of us want to feel, especially us girls? "In." *In* a group, to be an *in*sider, *in*cluded.

I get to hear a lot of girl drama. And this is what I've observed: most girl drama stems from feeling "out." Left *out*. There is something, especially inside a teenage girl, that longs for acceptance and fears rejection.

> As girls pull away from their parents, peers are everything . . . This is a time of deep searching for self in relationships. There is a constant experimenting—what reaction will I get from others? Talking to friends is a way of checking the most important question—Am I okay?[6]

> "Why do girls always travel in herds . . . ?" Do you travel in a herd with your girlfriends to the bathroom for example? Deep down there is something in you that travels in clusters because it "can give you a sense of security (I'm not alone)."[7]

We have a need to belong, to feel accepted, to feel "in." And because we want to feel "in" or accepted, we can easily find ourselves snuggled up in a comfy, cozy, curled-up faith.

Ever been so comfortable in a position that the last thing you wanted to do was budge? More than likely, when your alarm clock goes off at six thirty, waking you up for school, you are in such a comfy, cozy, curled-up position that you dread the thought of moving!

But when you have a comfy, cozy, curled-up faith, that means your heart is refusing to budge. The last thing it wants to do is move or change or grow, because moving and changing and growing can be uncomfortable.

Here are some characteristics of a passionate faith versus a comfy faith:

Comfy Faith:

- You live for God when others around you are living for God.
- You limit your talk of God to others who also believe in Him.
- You limit your time with God to just church or youth group activities.
- Deep down, you have given God some ultimatums: "Sure I'll follow You, unless . . ." You follow God until he interrupts a comfortable relationship, reputation, economic situation, or family life.
- You think about God only when you need something, such as a certain prayer to be answered.

Passionate Faith:

- You are the same on Sunday as you are on Monday.
- You talk about God with unbelievers.

- You live for God even if that means living contrary to what the crowd thinks is cool.
- You have committed your heart to God and are willing to follow Him no matter what happens in life—even if hurt happens, loneliness happens, or persecution happens.
- God is the first thing you think about in the morning, and He consumes your thoughts through every test, conversation, athletic practice. He is always on your heart.

Now check out your own heart. Are you more comfy or passionate in your faith? Explain. And then be honest with the question asked earlier. If you are bored with God, do you think you are bored by choice, because a comfy, lukewarm faith is more accepted by the world?

....

....

....

....

....

I used to focus more on acceptance, boys, and my reputation than I did my faith. I was focused on the tickets to popularity. What were those tickets? Juicy gossip, drama, drinking, dating, and smoking. And unfortunately, I paid for all of those tickets. Only, the price for those tickets scarred my heart more than my wallet.

Toward the end of high school, I finally started taking faith seriously. I was restless and hungry and wanted more from life than the boring, comfy faith I had. And I knew I had to do something about it, even if that meant rejection. So I climbed out of my comfy, cozy, curled-up faith and stepped out in bolder faith, daring to try to live like Jesus. It wasn't easy. I lost some friends, and I wasn't invited to as many parties. One of my closest friends stopped hanging out with me because I stopped attending the parties with all of our drinking friends.

Persecution doesn't have to look as extreme as prison walls. When we have a faith that's passionate, we will be persecuted, whether that means no saved seat at the lunch table, no invitation in the mail, or no homecoming crown.

Have you ever been persecuted for your faith? And if not, why not? If you aren't persecuted, could that be a sign that your faith is too comfortable, too boring?

We are so concerned with feeling accepted and "in" that we often have divided hearts—half seeking God's love and half seeking the world's love. But God wants your entire heart. Psalm 86:11 says, "Give me an undivided heart." Here are two beautiful verses to meditate on when you find yourself too concerned with what the world thinks of you.

Whoever comes to me I will never drive away.

—John 6:37

But now in Christ Jesus you who once were far away have been brought near through the blood of Christ.

—Ephesians 2:13

Through Jesus we are always "in" God's circle, always accepted by Him, always loved by Him. Keep that in mind when you feel isolated for living a life like Jesus—a life that may look strange to your friends.

Why Risk It?

A bride stripped of her wedding day, Moses ridiculed and criticized, Paul beaten and thrown out . . . why? Why would they risk it all for God?

Let's read Paul's words to find out:

I consider everything a loss compared to the surpassing greatness of knowing Christ Jesus my Lord, for whose

> sake I have lost all things. I consider them rubbish, that I may gain Christ and be found in him, not having a righteousness of my own that comes from the law, but that which is through faith in Christ—the righteousness that comes from God and is by faith. (Philippians 3:8–9)

According to this verse, Paul couldn't care less about love from the world! It was all rubbish to him! All that mattered was gaining Christ. And because of that, Paul was free to live a crazy, reckless, all-out, passionate faith that was far from boring. Sure it brought with it some weird looks, years in prison, and bruises . . . but he didn't care! And he had more joy because of it!

God wants your entire heart.

That's the kind of freeing faith I want—one that doesn't care about what anyone thinks. What about you? Maybe you want a boring faith because it brings you love from the world. Oh, but honey! God wants to free you from wanting acceptance from the world! It's in that freedom that you will find the life-giving, breathtaking, exhilarating faith that God created you for.

Going Deeper

God wants our hearts to be on fire with passion for Him. Mark 12:30 says, "Love the Lord your God with all your heart and with all your soul and with all your mind and with all your strength." Now read *The Message* translation of this verse: "Love the Lord God with all your passion and prayer and intelligence and energy."

A pastor named Rick Warren has some great insight on this verse. Read what he says about passion for God:

> Circle the word "passion." That word, in Greek, is the word "heart." God is saying I want you to put some muscle into it, put some energy, put some emotion into your relationship with Me. Don't be a wimp about your relationship with Me. Don't be namby-pamby. Don't be half-hearted. Give it all you've got.[8]

Never be lacking in *zeal*, but keep your spiritual fervor, serving the Lord.
—Romans 12:11, emphasis mine

Earlier I told you that our hearts are often divided, trying to please both the world and God. That gets in the way of a passionate, exciting faith. But what else gets in the way of your experiencing an unboring, passionate faith? Write some of your ideas here.

....

....

....

....

....

If we have a boring faith, it's our fault. To have a zealous faith, we have to want it, choose it, and then have the discipline to maintain it. Romans 12:11 says, "Keep your spiritual fervor." Rick Warren says that passion is "a discipline. It's not just automatic."[9] So what are some ways you can love the Lord your God with all your heart?

Here are some of my tips:

- Hang around friends who are passionate about Jesus! Ecclesiastes 4:9–10 says, "Two are better than one, because they have a good return for their work: If one falls down, his friend can help him up."

- Read about the God who is passionate about *you*! Why do you think we call the week of Jesus' crucifixion Passion Week? Because He is so passionate for you that He died for you! The more we see His passion for us, the more we find ourselves grateful for Him. (To find Scriptures about Passion Week, turn to the end of Matthew, Mark, Luke, and John.)
- Once you have spent time getting to know Jesus through His Word, live like Jesus did. When we imitate Jesus, we taste the life He lived. And His life was *anything* but boring.

To Sum It Up

Why do we get bored with God?

Being bored with God is more accepted by the world, and at times we feel a deeper need to be accepted by the world than by God.

Knowing this, how do we get unbored with God?

We have to see that it is a *choice* to be bored with God. When we love the world, we live a comfy, lukewarm faith. Hanging

out with friends who are passionate for Jesus, reading the Word and seeing how passionate God is for us, and then living the passionate life Jesus did will help take our faith from blah to awe.

6

Toss the Cap and Gown

The More We Know, the More We Don't Know

I couldn't get off the phone with him. To put it in chick-flick terminology: "He had me at hello." The first time I met him, I knew I could sit down with him at a coffee shop and spend hundreds of hours and dollars on conversation and lattes. There was something about him that drew me in. I was so curious to know everything. What was his family like? Did he like to chew gum? Was he good at sports? Bad dancer? Smart? What was his dream in life? Any fears? Did he wear braces in middle school? What were his thoughts on God? Did he wear Old Spice (because he smelled *sooo* good)?

And those were just a few of the thoughts banging around

in my brain about Brett Bishop. The man I would later commit my life to until death do us part.

To this day, I continually want to get to know Brett more. And I am always amazed at how much I *don't* know about him! I didn't know he liked coconut flavoring but hated actual coconut. I didn't know he liked chick flicks, or as he calls them, rom coms—short for romantic comedies. (Shh . . . don't tell him I told you that!) I didn't know that he would ever pick up ChapStick he found in a parking lot and use it (gross). I didn't know that he wakes up at seven thirty every morning—no matter how late he went to bed the night before. I didn't know how much he could challenge me in my faith, how he could love me more today than yesterday, or how clean he keeps his teeth. There are always new things I learn about Brett. And it's that wonder, that thought of continually learning about him and growing closer to him, that makes forever with him seem a short breath.

And then there's Shelley. The first time I met her, we cried together, we laughed together, we shared our hearts together, and we drank at least six glasses of Coca-Cola products together. After all, a four-hour, conversation-filled lunch requires multiple carbonated beverages to maintain strong energy and vocal cords. Yep. You read it correctly. I said *four-hour* lunch. Can I even call that lunch?

To this day, hours feel like minutes with Shelley. I love hearing her tell stories about growing up in Louisiana where football is a religion and people consume more red beans and rice than water. I love hearing about her global adventures of living in Israel, climbing Machu Piccu, and floating down the Nile River. I love that she asks me questions, is passionate about hot dogs, cries when she laughs, and isn't afraid to eat food that falls on the floor. There's always something new to discover, discuss, and delight in with Shelley. Life is an adventure with her.

Do you have a Brett or Shelley in your life? A friend who makes you feel loved and is easy to love back, a friend who makes an average day burst with color?

No matter if you find a Brett or not, if you have a Shelley or not, you and I will never have a relationship that is more romantic, more exciting, more curious and wonder-filled than our relationship with God when we decide to know Him in an intimate way. Every day you and I can learn about a side of God that we never knew before! Life is always an adventure when we share it with Him. We will *never* fully grasp Him.

In fact, the more you get to know God, the more you will realize how much you don't know about Him! And as we get to know more and more about Him, we feel more and more loved by Him. Just as my relationship with Brett grows the more I share my heart and learn about his, so our relationships with God deepen as we share life with Him.

Caps and Gowns

This life is all about graduating.

Think back to all of your graduation days. The day you graduated from kindergarten, elementary school, middle school, high school . . . What is the point of graduating? Besides buying a cute pair of shoes to show off while you walk across the stage, besides throwing the cap in the air, besides receiving a certificate or diploma. What is the real point?

We graduate to say we have completed that course of life, so bring on the next challenge!

A lot of times, we live this way. Some of us like the idea of completion, an item checked off the list, a goal met, so we can move on to the next one.

We live in a "been there and done that" society. We pride ourselves on being able to tell others that we've already been there, already done that, already graduated from that experience.

Experiment

What is that pride in us that loves to tell others that we've been there, done that? For some reason, it's a life competition between us girls, always needing to one-up each other. In fact, try a little experiment. The next time you are in a group of people, observe the conversation. Were there any "one-uppers"? Or maybe the one-upper is you. I know I have definitely tried standing taller than others. Let's try to be aware of how much we brag. And let's pray for others who do it too.

All Figured Out

Yes, we live in a world that loves to graduate. But there is an area in life that we will never be able to accomplish, complete, finish, or graduate from—our understanding of God.

Too bad we don't always believe that. Or should I be more specific—*I* don't always believe that.

I was the church girl, the one who knew all the Bible verses. The preacher's kid who could debate theological views. With a puffed-up chest and turned-up nose, I thought I knew all there was to know about God, and I judged others who didn't.

You may not be like I was or you may not be active in a youth group, Bible study, or church, but have you ever thought you knew all you needed to know about this God stuff? It makes sense if you have. We grow up around that sort of mindset. If we live in a society where you can accomplish almost anything, don't we get to a point where we think we have "accomplished" God? And isn't that one more answer to our "Why am I bored with God?" question? We get bored with God when we believe we have Him figured out.

I was reading another book about boredom with God the other day, and the author stated this truth: "If our students enroll in a growing relationship with God, they'll never want to graduate from it."[1] Isn't it cool to think that there will *never* be a day when you cannot learn something new about God and His ways? Just as I couldn't get off the phone with Brett or leave the lunch table with Shelley because of the endless exploration of each other's hearts, God asks us to explore Him.

What's More Exciting Than a Cardboard Box?

My friend Shelley has a five-year-old little boy named Micah. She told me that when he was a toddler, they noticed that at

Christmas Micah had more fun playing with the boxes his toys came in than with the toys themselves. So you know what she did? The next year she wrapped up an empty box. After all, that was all he played with the year before. Except *this* time, instead of playing with the box, Micah played with the bag they put the box in! Shelley couldn't win!

Don't you remember being a little girl and getting excited about the smallest things? An empty box, an ice-cream cone, a trip to the grocery store, a new tube of toothpaste (okay, so I still get excited about new toothpaste). Children look at the world with dancing eyes. That's the kind of wonder God desires from us.

I used to read the Bible stories about Daniel and the lions' den or God sending manna from heaven with those child-like eyes. But now I sometimes find myself reading with "flat" eyes. "We are exposed to a great danger today," writes Malcom McLeon, "the dying out of the sense of surprise."[2] And isn't that true? Why don't our eyes sparkle anymore?

How do we go from graduating from God to becoming amazed by God like a little girl on Christmas morning? Well, think about that and write some ideas down before I tell you what I think.

Wowed by His Wonder

Here are three ideas to help you have wonder-filled, jaw-dropping moments with God.

1. Below, I've listed some Bible stories—stories full of suspense, adventure, love, and happy endings. If you have read or heard these stories before, write down what you know about them—some of the major themes or life lessons that you remember. Then read the stories again and write down what you learn this time around. If you have never read or heard about these stories before, then have fun reading them for the first time! Write down your favorite verses and the key takeaways.
   - Queen Esther (Check out the whole book of Esther. It's short, and it's a great read!)
   - Noah and the Ark (This is found in Genesis 6–9.)
   - Jonah and the Great Fish (Jonah is another short book and an awesome read.)
   - Rahab the Prostitute and the Fall of Jericho (Joshua 2 and 6 tell Rahab's story, but read as many chapters in between as you want!)
2. Grab some friends and hit the hiking trails! Go outside. Get away from everyday life. Go to a local park or plan a camping trip. And then . . . stop. Stop and look at all the details in God's creation. Examine the different shapes of rocks, shades of leaves, and scents of flowers. Or simply stare up at the stars in your own backyard.
3. Get some extra education. Don't worry, I don't mean stay at school an extra hour. I mean take advantage

of the unlimited amount of YouTube videos, DVDs, books, and speakers that can take you to a deeper level of understanding about the universe, the history of the Bible, and the human body. Here are some personal favorites: Louie Giglio's *The Heart of Passion* on DVD, *Star of Bethlehem* (DVD), and Lee Strobel's books, such as *The Case for Faith* and *The Case for Christ*.

Going Deeper

Read the following verses. And as you read them, take note of what the writers did in their own lives or suggested that we do so that our knowledge and wonder of God expand. In fact, go ahead and circle the action words and the concepts these writers practiced or asked us to practice so that our faith never grows stagnant.

> Let me understand the teaching of your precepts; then I will meditate on your wonders.
>
> —Psalm 119:27

> Moses used to take a tent and set it up a long way outside the camp; he called it the "Meeting Tent." Anyone who wanted to ask the LORD about something would go to the Meeting Tent . . . The LORD spoke to Moses face to face as a man speaks with his friend. Then Moses would return to the camp, but Moses' young helper, Joshua son of Nun, did not leave the Tent."
>
> —Exodus 33:7, 11 NCV

The Spirit searches out all things, even the deep secrets of God. . . . we received the Spirit that is from God so that we can know all that God has given us.

—1 Corinthians 2:10, 12 NCV

Do your best to add these things to your lives: to your faith, add goodness; and to your goodness, add knowledge; and to your knowledge, add self-control; and to your self-control, add patience; and to your patience, add service for God; and to your service for God, add kindness for your brothers and sisters in Christ; and to this kindness, add love. If all these things are in you and are growing, they will help you to be useful and productive in your knowledge of our Lord Jesus Christ.

—2 Peter 1:5–8 NCV

Whoever has seen me has seen the Father.

—John 14:9 NCV

What can you glean from these verses that would help you deepen your knowledge of God and acknowledge just how limitless He is? Make a list of the helpful tips you learned through these verses.

....

....

I made my own list of discoveries. Compare your list to mine:

Psalm 119:27—Pray for a deeper understanding of God, and spend time thinking about all of God's miraculous works.

Exodus 33:7, 11—If I have questions about God, I shouldn't be afraid to sit and meet with God just like Moses did, face-to-face. And like Joshua, I need to spend *time* meeting with God. I shouldn't be in a hurry with God.

1 Corinthians 2:10, 12—The Holy Spirit knows everything about God, and that same Holy Spirit lives in me! Pray that the Holy Spirit will make God's heart known to me and that I will discern what the Spirit is trying to teach me about God.

2 Peter 1:5–8—Faith, goodness, knowledge, self-control, patience, service for God, kindness, and love will help me grow in my knowledge of God. Pray that God will help me in these areas. These are qualities that I can write down and put on my bathroom mirror to help me be more aware of them throughout my day. I will trust that by incorporating more of

these characteristics into my life, I will see what the heart of God is like.

John 14:9—By reading about the life of Jesus, I can get a glimpse of the heart of God.

So throw out the graduation cap and gown when it comes to God! He always has something new around the corner that will shake up that sleepy faith. Let's pray that God will give us a desire to seek more of His heart and never settle for where we are in our faith.

God, we thank You for how big You are. We confess that we get bored with You at times and need a deeper understanding of You. Would You help us see how wondrous You really are? Amen.

To Sum It Up

Why do we get bored with God?

Because there is something in us that believes we know it all—we know all there is to be known about God. We think we can spiritually graduate.

Knowing this, how do we get unbored with God?

We should model our hearts after Scripture and after the great men and women of faith we read about in God's Word. We should also hang out in nature and read Bible stories with new eyes, writing down all that we learn. And that's just the beginning. The more we get to know God, the more He will lead us to know Him—and our faith will become filled with childlike wonder.

7

Pruny Hearts

Jayabhai

Meet Jayabhai. She is a Marathi woman living in India. When she was just seventeen, her parents forced her to marry. More than likely, you are not too far from the age of seventeen. You could be seventeen right now. Imagine your parents picking out a husband for you and then kicking you out of the house around your junior or senior year of high school to live with a man you may not even know, much less love.

Maybe Jayabhai's arranged marriage would not have been so bad if her parents paired her with a man of integrity, but that was not the case.

"My parents got me married when I turned seventeen. I could not complete my secondary school certificate, as they were in a hurry to marry me to my uncle's son. They knew he was addicted to alcohol and yet got me married to him. Thus, my married life began with suffering that continued for five and a half years. Now as a widow with two daughters, ages five and three, to care for, I find myself even in more despair and hopelessness."

You might think that after her alcoholic husband died, her life would turn around, but in ancient Hindu custom (Hindu is the primary Indian religion), a widow has few options. "She can marry her husband's younger brother (if his family is willing); or, she can spend her remaining days in isolation in an *ashram*—a religious settlement—designed for widows, where she shaves her head, wears mourning clothes and seeks to 'atone' for her husband's death." Sometimes it's much worse. In the past, when a man died, the people would set his body ablaze atop a funeral pyre. The widow would then throw herself—or be forcibly thrown—atop the fire. This practice, known as *sati*, is now illegal, though it still happens in some rural areas. Widows are considered bad luck for families, so quite simply, they have no future.[1]

Although today these rules do not apply to every widow, a bleak future is still all too common for poorer widows and those who live in rural areas. Many widows in India turn into social rejects, begging for food on the side of the street. Some even turn to prostitution to buy themselves food. "With little social or economic status, many become destitute."[2]

Jayabhai faced this societal neglect at age twenty-three. But there are girls your age who face this twisted tradition. How do these girls ever have hope? Their identity is lost, and they have no future.

Jayabhai received hope and even peace for the first time because of the Word of God. The Bible Society of India (www.bsind.org)—whose mission is to make the Bible available to every person in India in a language he or she can understand—held a seminar for Indian widows organized by local churches. Jayabhai attended, not knowing what she was getting herself into.

The power of the Bible changed her life. Listen to her words. I think you will be shocked at what she says. (I know I was.)

"As I was going through the seminar, I was challenged by God to surrender the bitterness that I had against my parents, my husband and my sister-in-law to him. I struggled with this issue for more than a week. I also fortunately was given a Bible in my language—*Marathi*. As I read through the crucifixion, death and resurrection of Christ, I was able to forgive my people."[3]

What?! I would understand if she said something like, "Because I read the Bible, I know God loves me." Or "Because I read the Bible, I know God has a future for me." And I'm sure she does know that, but to read this quote about how the Bible gave her the ability to forgive her family . . . wow! Her parents wanted to get rid of her! They knew what they were doing when they sent her to live with an alcoholic. Then, after her husband died, Jayabhai had no one to care for her. It would take me years to forgive the jerks who did that to me!

But that quote is proof that the Bible is active. It is alive. It pierces hearts.

> **For the word of God is living and active. Sharper than any double-edged sword, it penetrates even to dividing soul and spirit, joints and marrow; it judges the thoughts and attitudes of the heart.**
>
> —Hebrews 4:12

Jayabhai saw God's heart in a new way. She saw the pain He went through to forgive her, to bring her into a relationship with Him. And it was only when Jayabhai saw the sacrificial heart of God that her own heart was changed.

Soak

That is the power of the Bible in someone's life. The Bible is what gives us "awe" in our faith because it teaches us about the heart of God.

Why do we find ourselves bored with God?

We don't know the Bible. Period.

This may not be your story. Maybe you are reading this book and you know the Bible like the back of your hand. But more than likely, if you are floundering in a shallow, boring faith, it's because you aren't soaking neck-deep in the Word of God.

What happens when you soak up the sun?

Your skin changes color.

What happens when you soak up lotion?

Your skin becomes smoother.

What happens when you soak up water?

Your skin gets pruny.

What happens when you soak up nacho cheese?

I don't know. But it would probably be gross, and you would lose all your friends.

My favorite part of taking a bath as a little girl was pruny fingers. I used to love how one minute my fingers would be smooth and the next minute they looked like little brains or fleshy-colored raisins. I used to wish my entire body would shrivel up in water just like my fingertips, but the older I got the more I realized that would just be really weird, and I was even weirder for wanting it in the first place.

Fun Fact

The outermost layer of the skin swells when it absorbs water. It is tightly attached to the skin underneath, so it compensates for the increased area by wrinkling. However, new research is investigating the role of digital vasoconstriction (narrowing of blood vessels) in the wrinkling of the skin due to water immersion.[4]

By the end of this book, I hope your heart is pruny because of all the time you spend soaking in Jesus—our Living Water. The more you soak up the truth of who God is, the more your heart will actually transform. It will go from smooth to pruny, from bored to floored.

Coffee Dates with God

One of the most important ways to live out your faith is by dedicating time to soaking up the Bible.

Every morning on my way to school, I would catch Dad in his study with a Bible in his lap. If he wasn't in there, his Bible would lie open in his favorite comfy armchair—a clue that told me he and God had had their regular morning coffee date. Occasionally, I have even walked past the room and caught a glimpse of Dad on his knees, with his head in his hands, talking to God. Although I never eavesdropped on their conversation, I knew he was praying for me. Every detail—my test that afternoon, my volleyball game later that evening, my relationships with friends, my future husband, and most of all my faith in God. No matter what morning it is—a Saturday morning, the ho-hum of a normal workday morning, a sad morning, a morning after little sleep—my dad will never miss his coffee date with God.

My mom used to grab me on my way out the door to school. "Mom! I don't have time!" I would whine. But my mom would say, "Honey, just one scripture. I'm going to read one scripture over you before you go to school." Little did I know that scripture would stick in my head as I went about my day. If I was stressed about a test, I would remember, "Do not be anxious about anything, but in everything . . . present your requests to God. And the peace of God . . . will guard your hearts and your minds in Christ Jesus" (Philippians 4:6–7).

In sixth grade I struggled with insomnia and this thing called obsessive-compulsive behavior. In my case, I had an obsessive routine before I went to bed. I had to have all my dresser drawers closed, my closet doors closed, all the bathroom lights out, the toilet lid down, and the shower door closed before I could even think about going to sleep. I would flip the light switch on and off, on and off, until I was convinced the lights were off for good. (That's when I started realizing something wasn't right. I mean, it's pretty obvious when a light is on or off, right?) Although it is difficult to put into words, the obsessive disorder took over my thoughts. I would replay any negative events of the day, maybe a hurtful conversation with a friend or an embarrassing moment in the cafeteria, over and over in my head until I could mentally travel through the scene and picture every detail just the way it happened and then re-create what I should have said or what I should have done. I would do this every night while I lay in bed, replaying thoughts until I broke out in cold sweats. I would stay awake half of the night.

It was my first year of middle school, and my life was out of control! Peer pressure, loneliness, insecurities . . . and it was my need to be in control that brought on my obsessive-compulsive tendencies. The obsessive-compulsive tendencies interrupted my sleep, sending me to school with even more stress. And the nasty cycle continued . . . stress—control freak—obsessive-compulsive girl—no sleep—stress—control freak—obsessive-compulsive girl . . . you get the point.

I remember my mom lying next to me, night after night, as I tried to shake the plague of thoughts and tossed and turned in my bed. She would comb her fingers through my hair and whisper Scripture over me until my body would finally give up. Something in me would let go, and sleep would finally take over. To this day, I know it was the power of God's Word that brought healing to my mind and, most of all, my heart. Peace, unexplainable peace, kicked stress off of its throne and began to rule my life—it was the peace my mom begged God for night after night after night.

Why did I go into all this?

Because my mom and dad not only have faith, they *live* faith. And living out faith is one of the keys to spiritual adventure! One of the most important ways to live out your faith is by dedicating time to soaking up the Bible.

My parents have chosen to daily hold God's hand through the bad, the good, and the ordinary. They have chosen to meet with God on a daily basis by opening up God's Word and then applying it to their lives.

Notice that I used the word *chosen*. It's not that they always *feel* like hanging out with God. It's not that they are always jumping up and down at the thought of opening up the Bible. Some days they long to sit with Him, and other days it can feel like a routine or habit. But no matter how they feel, they are committed. It's through this commitment that they get to know God for who He is. And it's through this commitment that they can honestly say, "God's love surprises me more and more every morning."

When you and I choose to commit to this God thing—when we choose to have a coffee date, a lunch date, or even a nighttime hot cocoa date with Him on a daily basis, His love will surprise us too.

Is the Bible an Awkward First Date?

Soaking up who God is through the Bible will leave you in complete and utter wonder. But let's get real. Sometimes reading the Bible can feel like an awkward first date! You open it up, stare at it, not sure what it is saying and completely unsure of how to get to know it. But let me tell you—as one who has faced that first-date awkwardness with the Bible—once you give it time by asking it questions, listening to it, and looking at it, you start getting to know it. It becomes your counselor and your guide, nourishing your soul with what you crave.

During my junior year of high school, my spiritual life finally came alive for the first time like never before. I had decided to dive into the Bible, not just once or when I felt like it, but to sit with it on a consistent basis and soak in each word. Did I always feel like reading my Bible? No. But I began to notice that every time I chose the Bible over something else, I drew a little closer to God's heart. Pretty soon it became a familiar old friend.

Pruning Our Hearts

I know, in my life, if I am ever bored with God, it's because I'm not taking the time to explore His vastness and get lost in His love. So when you take daily time to get to know God through His Word, I think you will see a change in the way you see Him. In fact, I *know* you will because He promises it! Read it for yourself:

I am the true vine, and my Father is the gardener. He cuts off every branch in me that bears no fruit, while every branch that does bear fruit he prunes so that it will be even more fruitful. You are already clean because of the word I have spoken to you. Remain in me, and I will remain in you. No branch can bear fruit by itself; it must remain in the vine. Neither can you bear fruit unless you remain in me.

—John 15:1–4

Okay, so the pruning talked about in this verse isn't the same pruny-ness we were talking about in the bathtub, but they can go hand in hand.

FUN FACT

What is *pruning* a plant?

1 : to cut off or cut back parts of for better shape or more fruitful growth

2 : to cut away what is unwanted or superfluous[5]

If you stay connected to God, soaking Him up through His Word, your heart gets filled with His goodness—it gets *pruny* with goodness. And your heart loses all its rough edges and junk—it gets *pruned*. For example, I struggle with giving money—lending to a friend, offering to buy a meal, even giving to the homeless. I'm pretty stingy. And this stinginess is just the type of junk that God wants to prune. He has slowly been cutting off my gross money-hoarding tendency with this verse found in 1 John 3:17–18: "If anyone has material possessions and sees his brother in need but has no pity on him, how can the love of God be in him? Dear children, let us not love with words or tongue but with actions and in truth."

Have you ever read a Scripture that pruned your heart—took out some of the bad parts? If so, write about it.

The way the Bible prunes our hearts proves that its words are powerful, that they are alive and active.

Is the Bible Really *Alive*?

When you hear people say that the Bible is alive, you may picture a Bible with eyes, little legs, and little arms singing that old Sunday school song, "The B-I-B-L-E." (Or maybe that mental picture only pops up in my crazy head.) But the Bible's words really are alive and active, transforming (pruning) hearts and minds to help us experience the unboring life God desires for us.

Deuteronomy 32:47 says, "They are not just idle words for you—they are your life." According to this verse, what are God's words?

Life! God's words are life! If this "life" still seems a little vague to you, let's take a look at some real girls who have experienced real life through the active and alive words of the Bible.

Laura

I was a sophomore in high school. I'll never forget the note that Ben passed me in second period English class as he said, "Laura, we want you to sign up! A bunch of your friends did."

Ben was one of the "cool guys" and was pretty mean to a lot of people. That made me cautiously wonder what kind of sign-up sheet he could possibly want to recruit me to be a part of. I opened the folded-up piece of lined paper and, at first glance, noticed a few of my girlfriends' names scribbled in their handwriting on the page, mixed in with several more of the popular guys in my class. My eyes scrolled from bottom to top, and it was at the top that I saw what the sign-up was for. The title read: "Friends with Benefits." I could feel my face turning red as I quickly looked back at Ben to see if he was being serious or if this was some stupid joke. He had a little half smile on his face and tried to persuade me, "Come on—it's just for fun. No strings attached!"

At that moment I felt backed into a corner. No way was I going to put my name on that ridiculous piece of paper. On the other hand, I could practically feel the pressure of the cool guys physically weighing down on me. I turned around and looked Ben in the eye as I tore the paper up and said, "I hope you know not to ever ask me something like this again." I looked back at the front of the classroom as I thought, *Here we go.*

I had felt myself pulling away from my ring of girlfriends for the past two years. We were all really close in junior high and, for the most part, held the same values and had the same interests. Starting in about ninth grade, however, I noticed that our group of five was beginning to fragment. My best friend and I stuck together, while the other three tried some things we weren't comfortable with—sampling alcohol, getting physical with guys. They were just different. The names of those three girls had been on that paper, and I knew Ben would be telling them that I objected to their absurd game.

Sure enough, by the end of the day, I was a "prude" and "boring." One of my former friends even told me I was judgmental and too churchy. My friendship with the three girls was over from that point on. They totally kicked me out of their social gatherings and made me the butt of all their jokes, determined to make sure the cool guys knew they were not my friends. That day started off three months of rumors, meanness, and isolation.

I was so conflicted! I asked God why I should ever "do the right thing" if this were the result of my obedience to what I felt was pleasing to Him. It didn't seem like standing up for good was really paying off. One evening when I was reading my Bible, I came across 1 Peter 4:15–16: "If you suffer, however, it must not be for murder, stealing, making trouble, or

> prying into other people's affairs. But it is no shame to suffer for being a Christian. Praise God for the privilege of being called by his name!" (NLT).
>
> Every time I had read that verse before, it seemed disconnected to my life. What do I know of suffering? But that night, these verses clicked with me because I felt that my last three months had been marked by true emotional suffering. You suffer for wrongdoing—yeah, that makes sense. But if someone is giving you grief for looking like Christ in the way you live—that's a sign you're doing something *right*! And God is smiling down on you, welling up with pride because people are pointing their fingers at you, calling you "Christian." The name-calling won't last forever, but it's nothing to be ashamed of if the name they're calling you is "Christ."

What did Laura learn about God's heart in 1 Peter 4:15–16? That He delights in us when we stand up for Him. When everyone else thinks we are crazy, God doesn't because we have taken on *His* name!

How did that realization about God change Laura? It made her care less about what others think about her and, instead, focus on God's approval, even if it's not the popular thing to do.

How did that change help Laura experience true life? Laura started seeing life with an eternal perspective. She had a choice: Care about what others call her in this short life. Or care about what God would call her forever. Laura chose to live for God and not her peers. I don't know about you, but when I have that peer pressure and the pressure of living up to everyone else's standards off my back, then a heavy weight has been lifted off my shoulders. I can breathe again! I'm less paranoid. I feel free! Now *that* is *life*, baby!

Going Deeper

Analyze the following story about how the Bible is active in our lives, giving us life.

Amanda

After I graduated college, everything was looking great. Only a few months later I was offered a teaching position. My best friend got a job in the same town as I did, and we were going to be roommates. I was in love with an amazing Christian man, whom I was certain God had placed in my life.

But as soon as the new school year started, things went downhill fast. The school where I taught was extremely difficult. I literally went home crying every day. Instead of going to God, I began to cry on the phone every night to my boyfriend, who was currently living in another state. I began unloading all my burdens onto him, which was not healthy for our relationship. I began to elevate him above God, because I felt like he could save me from this situation. I felt alone in a new city, with few friends and a job that overwhelmed me.

Finally Thanksgiving came, and I took a well-deserved break. I went up to visit my boyfriend, and he took me ring shopping. I just knew that this ring would rescue me from my horrible predicament.

When Christmas came, somebody got a ring! But it was not me. It was my best friend and roommate. A few weeks later I got something too—a phone call from my boyfriend, ending our relationship. I was probably at the lowest point in my life. I had rested all of my hope on a person who let me down. That was when God showed me where my hope should always remain—in Him.

I was completely broken, and God came in and picked me up. I had been neglecting my relationship with Him for so long. To this day I feel as though God cleared out everything in my life just so that He could fill it back up with Himself. While my heart was breaking, God revealed Himself to me in Psalm 46.

Verse 5 especially spoke to my heart. It said, "God is within her, she will not fall." I quoted this daily and even hourly sometimes. No matter the situation that I was in, God would get me through it if I relied on Him. He gave me strength to make it through the school year. He gave me joy for my roommate who was getting married. He gave me support through a Bible study group that I got plugged in to. He did not let me fall.

What did Amanda learn about God's heart in the Psalm 46 verse?

How did that realization about God change Amanda?

How did that change help Amanda experience true life?

Bored with God? Spend time soaking up His Word! It will prune your heart, taking out the junk that keeps you from experiencing the true life God wants to give you. And then apply the verses to your life as Laura and Amanda did. Just like them, you will experience a closeness with God that is life changing.

I know you still might be reading this thinking, *Okay, Jenna, but seriously, the Bible is just so boring to read!* I believe boredom comes from lack of understanding. If you think the Bible is boring, you don't understand its powerful story. In the next chapter, we are going to understand just how beautiful this story is, so maybe you will actually *want* to open it.

To Sum It Up

Why do we get bored with God?

We don't spend time soaking in the Bible.

Knowing this, how do we get unbored with God?

Spend daily time in His Word. When we do that, it prunes away the gross parts of our hearts that get in the way of us experiencing the life God wants us to live. When we apply Scripture to our lives, we experience an alive, active, unboring relationship with Him.

8

A Very *Un*boring Story

My favorite part about a movie or a good book is a clean, joyful, hopeful, happy ending. It's that moment where you find yourself just . . . smiling. Do you ever catch yourself doing that? It's that sigh of relief during the final movie score melody. It's when your eyes get watery with happy tears as you turn to that final chapter. You've connected to the characters. You've walked with them through the desert so that you could rejoice with them when she fell in love, or he found the buried treasure, or they had a baby, or she was healed, or he got married, or . . . you get my point.

Would a story be good if there weren't a serious problem to overcome? No! We love a plot that takes us into the trenches with the characters. Why? Because it makes a happy ending that much happier! We cannot appreciate a Disneyesque happily-ever-after ending without a wicked stepmother, witch, or scary underwater octopus. (If you know which Disney villain was an octopus, then you now know the most-watched Disney movie in the Lucado house growing up.)

The Bible *is* that story, the *greatest* story! And that's why soaking it up takes us on a God-discovering adventure that leaves us wanting more. It gives us drama, betrayal, suspense. But most of all, the Bible tells us about the greatest love story ever told. Who has the leading role? God, of course (and we will include Jesus and the Holy Spirit within that role, since they are all one). And who has the supporting role in this story? Drum roll, please . . .

It's *you*!

And who doesn't want to read a good love story, especially if you're the one being loved? If you're bored with God, then you don't understand the beautiful love story of the Bible.

> **Story is the language of our hearts.**
>
> **—Brent Curtis and John Eldredge, *The Sacred Romance*[1]**

As little girls, most all of us loved to not only listen to stories, but also to pretend we were a part of the story. And if we were honest, we would all admit that there is still something in us that longs to be a part of a good romance or to be the heroine in a good drama. I believe this longing to be in a story points to something deep within us. Something inside that hopes life is not just a random series of events, but is part of a greater story. Otherwise we would have no purpose. The Bible reveals to us that our lives are no accident; they do have purpose and meaning. We are chosen characters in an eternal story "that God has been weaving since before the beginning of time, which he has also placed in our hearts."[2]

In the following passage, you will get a small glimpse of what the overarching story of the Bible has looked like in my life. It gives you a hint of my testimony and how the gospel changed my life. The "gospel" is the crux of the Bible. The story I wrote gives you a taste of how the gospel comes to life in our hearts and imaginations as we soak up Scripture. Our story becomes a part of the bigger story when we read the Bible.

(What you are about to read is in "Jenna language," but it is a story based on biblical truth. I've included the scriptural inspirations so you can take some time to check them out.)

A Master's Piece of Art

This story opens up in a sewing room.

But not just any sewing room.

This is a heavenly sewing room. God's favorite place to create.

This particular day, the sewing room was bursting at the seams with the wings of angels, who were crowding together to see the new masterpiece.

"Is it a son or a daughter?" asked one of the angels.

"A daughter," God said with the proud smile of a new Father.

Another angel noticed God sewing together the most important part of this new daughter—her heart.

"Oooooh! What will she look like?" (Although on earth this question would be answered by listing attributes of the physical, in heaven this question is answered by listing attributes of the internal. After all, God looks at the heart first—1 Samuel 16:7.)

"Well, I will give her a heart like her mother, Denalyn, sensitive and compassionate. And like her dad, Max, I will give her a desire to teach others about Me." As God spoke the words, He stitched her heart together one thread at a time (Psalm 139:15).

"And what will her earthly name be?" another angel inquired.

"Well, let Me show you." God held out His big Papa palm, big enough to hold the universe. And on the palm were all of the names of all His children. Freshly inscribed was the name "Jenna" (Isaiah 49:16).

"I can't wait to meet her! And what will her tent look like?" (In heaven, the angels call human bodies "tents" because they know they are temporary camping sites that house humans only until they finally live in their eternal homes—2 Corinthians 5:4.)

"Oh, she will be magnificent like all of My children," God said with a sigh of satisfaction. "Beautifully and wonderfully made; unique in her own way. Wavy, golden-brown hair, with almond-shaped eyes. Her ears will look like her great-grandmother Roberta's. And her chin will resemble that of her grandfather Jack. In fact, hurry and grab Roberta. I'm sure she would love to watch Me sew her great-granddaughter in her own granddaughter's womb. And go ahead and grab the rest of the family while you're at it" (Psalm 139:14–15).

So the angels called Roberta and all the relatives who had gone home before Jenna. Then . . . the fun part.

They watched.

Watched as God did one of the things God does best—stitch.

He started with her inmost being, stitching her soul. Then, working His way out, He stitched her mind and her tent together one thread at a time in His very image (Genesis 1:27).

"There," God said with tears of joy in His eyes. "Isn't she lovely?"

And the angels worshiped the Creator. Another work of art. Another masterpiece.

But it wouldn't take long before God's tears of joy would turn into tears of pain.

"We will just see how long this celebration lasts," hissed the Dark Angel.

The Dark Angel had fallen from God long ago and now lived only to ruin God's art. Creation days for him were nothing but a challenge—a challenge to turn the art from her Creator, unravel her thread, leaving her broken and ashamed (Isaiah 14:12–14).

"If I can whisper lies to Jenna, telling her she is of no worth, no beauty, no significance—if I can distract her from her Creator, she will be mine." The Dark Angel cracked a malicious grin and put his plan into action.

Jenna turned her back on her proud Papa (Isaiah 53:6). She went from singing songs to Him on her swing set to singing the praises of popularity, worshiping worldly possessions, and idolizing anything that would give her the love and attention of man, while forgetting her biggest Fan. And slowly, the strings that held her together began to unravel.

Like all of His children, Jenna went from knowing she was a masterpiece to comparing her work of art to others. She compared her intellect, her athletic ability, and her body to everyone else's. And because she began to devalue her art, she abused it—watching movies and television that hurt her eyes, listening to songs that damaged her ears, saying words that poisoned her tongue, thinking thoughts that soured her mind. She even gave threads of her art away, thinking it would help her love herself again, when instead it devalued her even more. And slowly, the threads that held her together unraveled even more.

It seemed the plans of the Dark Angel were working.

"Why?" the angels cried to God. "Why does she not know who You made her to be? Why does she not see her value?"

"The Dark Angel is at work," God said.

"Why do You let him lie to her?" the angels asked, knowing what God would say.

"You know I give My masterpieces a choice—to know My love and love Me in return or to reject My love. Give her time, my angels. She does not know My love because she does not know the Son" (Romans 3:22).

"But hasn't she heard about the Son?" the angels asked.

"Yes, but the Son cannot stitch her back together until she sees her strings coming undone (Psalm 51:17). Jenna has not seen her brokenness. Be patient. It takes a while for My children to see their sin, and Jenna is well on her way. The Dark Angel has turned her to the world, and the world has worn her down. But she will soon remember her Creator."

It took seventeen years.

Seventeen years for the daughter to see the strings of her heart unraveled. Maybe it was the moments after drinking too much. Maybe it was the moments after she gossiped about her closest friend. Maybe it was the moments after lying to her parents. Maybe it was the moments after calling her sisters cutting names. Shame does that. Shame loosens heartstrings. And when Jenna saw her shame, when she saw her loose strings, coiled knots, and unraveled heart, she finally asked the Son to make her new (2 Corinthians 5:17).

And He did. Oh, how He did! He stitched her back together, this time with new thread—a thread that comes from Himself.

This thread has colors that bring life as you have never seen it before (John 10:10)! This thread is so soft it comforts all sadness (2 Corinthians 1:3). And the peace! Oh, the peace that these untangled strings bring (Philippians 4:6–7)! Even more important, these are the only threads that cannot unravel. Why? Because they belong to the Son, and the Son holds all strings together (Colossians 1:17). Sure, Jenna has knotted them and twisted them a little, and just today, after forgetting how much her Papa loves her, she split yet another one. (This happens quite often.) But the Son secures the strings with a tight promise that will never leave her unraveled like before (John 10:28).

What is the promise?

God so loved His children that He sent his one and only Son to live on the earth (John 3:16). His Son lived a perfect life, knot- and tangle-free, no loose string to be found. He lived the perfect life that God's children cannot live, yet He died the death that unraveled lives deserve. The Son wrapped

Himself up in the world's unraveled strings of sin (Isaiah 53:6)—strings of sexual impurity, strings of selfishness, strings of anger and bitterness, strings of cheating and lying, strings of murder and adultery—and wore them. He wore them all the way to the cross where He died.

But why? Why did the Son have to die?

So that the art wouldn't have to. The punishment for sin is death (Romans 6:23). The Son took on the punishment and also defeated it. Three days after dying on the cross, He rose from the dead.

And when He rose, the world's knots and unraveled strings were defeated (1 Corinthians 15:3–4). That way, when Jenna saw her brokenness, when she saw her strings in a pile on the floor, she knew whose name to call. And when she did, the Son was waiting, waiting to forgive her, waiting to love her, waiting to be in a relationship with her, and waiting to stitch her into a masterpiece even more beautiful and new than before (Romans 10:9).

"You know, my Lord," one of the angels commented, "her chin may still resemble her Grandpa Jack's, and her ears may still look like Great-Grandmother Roberta, but I have to say, her heart is looking more and more like the Son!"

"That's the beauty of My love," God replied with pride, a pride that lit up the heavens. "When My daughter trusts in the Master to piece her back together, then she becomes more than a masterpiece of art; she becomes the Master's piece of art I called her to be."

At that, the proud Papa picked up a new thread.

"Who are you stitching together now?" an angel asked with excitement.

> "Another beautiful work of art. Her name will be ________________(insert your name here)."

This is the gospel. The Bible is far from boring. It is a story—a story with a villain, a hero, a damsel in distress. And the more we soak up this story, the more unboring our faith will be. You are a part of this eternal story! Isn't that cool to think about? It creates purpose, gives you identity, and makes your faith so much more exciting! Let's take a closer look at your character and God's character within the gospel story:

- You were *created* by a perfect Father. God designed the freckles on your nose and the dimples on your cheeks. He knows the number of hairs on your head. He knows you. He loves you.
- You have *turned away* from the Father. (And don't read that in an accusatory tone, because I am right there with ya, sister!) I don't care if you have gone to church your entire life and have always followed the rules. Turning from God means doing anything against His desire for our lives. Even if that means complaining because you don't want to get out of bed, not sharing a shirt with your sister, or thinking judgmental thoughts about another girl's outfit. We have *all* sinned. We have *all* turned away. Some sins may be loud and obvious. Others may be quieter and hiding in dark corners.
- Your sin *separates* you from God. Why? Because God is a good, perfect, and holy God—who is also just.

> And because He is just, He has to punish our wrong. That makes sense, right? I mean, you wouldn't want a judge telling the murderer, "Don't worry about it, buddy. Have a nice day." No! We want to see justice! And we have a God who is all about justice. But you know what that means, right? That our sinful selves are on trial. The punishment our sin deserves is death (Romans 6:23). Yep. You and I are sitting on death row.

Remember how we thought about the beauty of happy endings? And what did we conclude? That an ending isn't memorable, climactic, or goose bump–worthy unless there is a problem.

In this story, we aren't the superhero or the comic relief.

We are the problem. We are the drama. We are the reason the ending to this story is so good. (Refer back to the reality of our hearts without Jesus in chapter 2.)

But it cannot be good unless you see yourself for who you are. You have to reach a point where you know you are broken. You have to see your sin. You have to admit you are stuck.

I didn't get unbored with God until I realized how desperate my character was in the gospel story.

Why do you struggle with seeing your need for God? If you don't feel desperation for a Savior, why do you think that is?

....

....

....

....

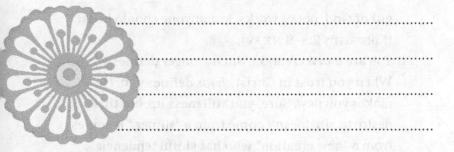

Don't worry. I won't leave the story hanging. To close out the chapter, let's close out your story.

- Jesus is *your* Savior! He offers more than bleach, more than a mop and bucket to clean us and make us new. He offers Himself to save us from ourselves. And it looks like this: "God made him who had no sin to be sin for us, so that in him we might become the righteousness of God" (2 Corinthians 5:21). Jesus took our place. There was a heart swap! He took our messy ones and gave us His clean one. And He doesn't ask us to dust or vacuum our junky hearts. No. He takes on our dirty messes without requiring anything from us. So many of us believe that God will forgive us if we clean ourselves up, or if we go to church every Sunday and don't talk back to our parents. But it has nothing to do with what *we do* and has everything to do with what *Christ did*!
- You *trust* Jesus. Believe that Christ's death is enough to clean you and make you new. And because He loves you, by His grace you are promised eternal life. Check this out: "By grace you have been saved through faith, and that not of yourselves; it is the

gift of God, not of works, lest anyone should boast" (Ephesians 2:8–9 NKJV).

- You are a *new* creation. Sin no longer defines you! When you trust in Christ, *Jesus* defines you. He makes you new. Sure, you still mess up, but this desire to sin doesn't come from a "sinner," it comes from a "new creation" who has sinful tendencies.

Now that's what I call a happy ending!

Going Deeper

Read some of the names God calls you once you give your heart to Jesus. I have a feeling you will feel a lot better about your character in this story after reading about who God has made you to be through Jesus.

God's Possession (1 Corinthians 6:20)
Child of God (John 1:12)
Precious Jewel (Malachi 3:17)
Beloved (Romans 1:7; 2 Thessalonians 2:13)
Complete (Colossians 2:10)
Loved Eternally (Jeremiah 31:3)

I know these names tell you a lot about you, but based on the gospel story you read and the names that He gives you, what is something new you learned about God's character?

....

....

Jesus is the hero in this story. And if you have never put your trust in the Hero to save you, this is the time. You don't have to confess your new belief to a priest or call your pastor. You can do it right now! If you need to know how to tell God that you want to trust Him, you can pray along with this prayer:

Father, I've messed up. I have a dirty heart that needs a major cleaning job. I believe that Jesus came down to earth and died on the cross for my sins. I believe that He is the Son of God. And because I believe that, I want to ask You to make me new. Please forgive me. Please enter into my heart and change me. Help me with this new journey with You. Thank You for loving me enough to die for me. Amen.

To Sum It Up

Why do we get bored with God?

We don't understand the depths of the story that is in the Bible. The gospel is the crucial story the Bible gives us. And within it we find that our lives are not just accidental, but are part of a beautiful drama that God has designed from the beginning.

Knowing this, how do we get unbored with God?

We can spend more time reading the story of the Bible and applying the story to our lives. We can ask God to show us how desperate our characters are for a hero so that our hearts will appreciate and love God more. And we can look at the character of God more. The more we understand, the less bored we will be.

9

A New Zip Code

Hey, lady, I got here first."

"I don't care if you got here first. My daughter has been sick for weeks."

"Oh yeah? You try living with a demonic husband!"

A line of people wrapped around Simon's house. Word was out. Everyone wanted to meet this new miracle worker in town. Rumor had it that earlier that day, this new guy cast a demon out of the town lunatic. Now Mr. Looney was Mr. Normal.

"What happened to him?" the townspeople asked as they passed the once-demon-possessed man. His hair had gone from matted to soft, his eyes from frantic to sparkling, and his voice from shrill to calm.

"I don't know. I heard some guy named Jesus put a spell on him."

"I heard that he cast a demon out of him."

Whispering and murmuring filled the streets as the townspeople of Capernaum spread the name of Jesus faster than gossip in the cafeteria.

"I also heard that this Jesus dude taught in the synagogue and didn't put everyone to sleep like Rabbi Benjamin."

"Ha! No napping in the synagogue? That's almost harder to believe than driving out demons!"

His teaching, His miracles, His authority—Jesus had barely been in Capernaum a full day before He was leaving a God-sized imprint.

> That evening, after the sun was down, they brought sick and evil-afflicted people to him, the *whole city* lined up at his door! He cured their sick bodies and tormented spirits.
>
> —Mark 1:32–33 MSG, emphasis mine

Talk about instant popularity! It takes a handful of hours for Jesus to be the buzz of the town, for people to literally line up to see Him. They knew Jesus had something they didn't. A power they hadn't seen before, a message they hadn't heard before. When Jesus spoke, shivers climbed up spines, tears ran down cheeks, smiles spread across faces. "Mark wishes us to know . . . that Jesus constantly filled people with a mixture of wonder, awe and fear at what he said and did," writes Donald English. [1]

Check out the townspeople's reactions in the verses below.

Everyone there was incredulous, buzzing with curiosity.

—Mark 1:27–28 MSG

They were surprised at his teaching—so forthright, so confident—not quibbling and quoting like the religion scholars.

—Mark 1:22 MSG

Jesus taught in a way that was not boring! It was a style of teaching they had never heard before. What was He saying? We will never know exactly, but we know it had something to do with the Kingdom of God (Mark 1:15). "Jesus preached the good news of the kingdom of God. He told people that the world . . . was the place where God was making salvation, where every person was a creature loved by God and chosen by him for the grandest of purposes."[2]

Using some of the adjectives from Mark 1, describe the people's reaction to Jesus.

....

....

....

....

Did your answer include the word "bored"?

Mine didn't. Scripture says these people were "buzzing," "surprised," "curious." These people had tasted something sweet, and they wanted more.

Why do you think these people and so many others in the Bible were in awe of Jesus? Sure, He worked a miracle in front of them, but it's something deeper than that. Who He was, what He said, the life He lived went beyond the head and into hearts. These people heard a message and saw a man who had set off an alarm in the deepest parts of themselves. Something was different about Him. He had something their hearts wanted. What did their hearts want?

A new zip code.

A New Zip Code

If you have ever moved before, you will know that two major things happen. Number one, you move into a new culture. The neighborhood is different, people are different, trends are different. New smells, new sights, new ways of doing things. Number two, you move into a new home. That home could be a house, an apartment, or a duplex. You might also have a new family dynamic with this new home—maybe Mom and Dad have separated, maybe Grandma has moved in. When Jesus came, He offered people a chance to move—move out of the kingdom they were in and into a new one.

There are two kingdoms: the one in which humans, possessions, and essentially the world rules your heart; and the Kingdom Jesus preached about—the one in which God rules your heart.

Jesus' message then and His message today is the same: "'The time promised by God has come at last!' he announced. 'The Kingdom of God is near! Repent of your sins and believe the Good News!'" (Mark 1:15 NLT).

Kingdom of God? Sound foreign? Well, to help you understand, here's a short exploration of this new Kingdom life. (This is a simple way of describing the new Kingdom that a group called Think Orange published. Check it out. I think you'll like it.)

"Our Father in heaven, hallowed be your name, your *kingdom* come, your will be done on earth as it is in heaven" (Matthew 6:9–10, emphasis mine).

Okay, not trying to bore you here, but to understand this verse, let's break down the language a little. You can't necessarily see this from the English translation, but in the original text, Jesus used a really interesting literary tool. He uses something we call parallelism.

Parallelism is like saying the same thing twice but using different words. So Jesus was saying, "Your Kingdom come = Your will being done." Basically, someone's will and someone's kingdom are linked together; God's will and God's Kingdom are connected.

Jesus' message was, "I am bringing God's way of doing things into a world where things have gone terribly wrong. God's way is coming." Essentially, Jesus Himself was a walking example of what God's Kingdom would look like. By living a blameless life, He was saying, "If you want to know what God looks like, it's Me. If you want to see what God's Kingdom looks like, watch Me."[3]

Just like when you move to a new town and the culture changes, when you move into God's Kingdom, you experience a brand-new way of living. In Kingdom living, God rules your heart. When God rules your heart, you live the way He wants you to live. How do we know the way He wants us to live? We look at Jesus. We look at what the Bible says. When we are "Kingdom girls," we live the Jesus way and we use the Bible as our guide. With that being said, it's thinking time.

Write down what a "Kingdom girl" looks like. Give some examples of what your everyday culture would look like if you changed zip codes—moved into God's Kingdom. To help you out, I'm going to provide some examples from Jesus' life. After reading each verse, write down how you can model His behavior in your own life.

> But when the teachers of religious law who were Pharisees saw him eating with tax collectors and other sinners, they asked his disciples, "Why does he eat with such scum?"
>
> —Mark 2:16 NLT

....

....

So he got up from the table, took off his robe, wrapped a towel around his waist, and poured water into a basin. Then he began to wash the disciples' feet, drying them with the towel he had around him.

—John 13:4–5 NLT

He went up into the hills by himself to pray.

—Matthew 14:23 NLT

I'm not saying you have to put a towel around your waist, find a hill in order to pray, or find an IRS agent to eat dinner with. That's not the point of these verses. When we read about Jesus, we not only look at what He does, but we also look at the heart behind the actions.

In these verses, we see a serving heart, a heart for the hurting, a heart that draws near to God. This is but a small example of what Kingdom living is like. It's living a life with a heart that models Jesus' heart. And girl, that kind of life is *not* boring! When we look at Jesus, do we see a man with insecurities, people-pleasing problems, materialistic tendencies, or a life full of drama? No! We see the essence of joy, peace, and love. We see a life that the deepest parts of our hearts long for. And you can have it when you choose this new zip code. So this new culture models Jesus. Another guide to this new life is found in the Word of God.

Reading a Recipe

If I'm cooking dinner, I will usually pull out a recipe, read through it, and then follow the instructions. What would happen if I read the recipe and didn't follow its instructions? *Well, duh, Jenna, you would still be hungry.* Right! So why don't we apply that simple methodology when reading the Bible?

We can soak up the Bible, memorize Scriptures, circle and highlight our favorite passages, but when it comes to *doing* what the Bible says to do . . . well . . . that's a different story. Do we want to be filled, taste the goodness of God, and experience a transformation in our lifeless souls? If your soul isn't boiling with excitement about God, then here is my question for you: Are ya reading the Bible *and* doing what it says to do? Because until we actually read the Bible *and* follow its instructions, we won't taste what this new, awe-inspiring Kingdom life is all about.

James 1:22 tells us to "be *doers* of the word, and not hearers only, *deceiving* yourselves" (NKJV, emphasis mine). Why do you think that if you don't do what the Bible says, you would be deceiving yourself?

I like the way John Stott puts it in his commentary. He says, "We deceive ourselves when we mistake the part for a whole."[4] See, hearing the Word of God is only part of its purpose.

A lot of people think doing what the Bible says or being a Christian just looks like a lot of rules to check off.

Don't cheat. Check.

Don't envy. Check.

Don't lust. Check.

Have you ever felt that way?

Dirty Bowls

Let's say I invite you over for dinner tonight. Soup is on the menu, so I set out some bowls and tell you to go ahead and serve yourself. When you pick up the bowl, you notice that the inside of the bowl looks dirty.

"Uh, Jenna? I think this bowl isn't clean. There's some leftover food kinda crusted to the inside," you tell me, while showing me the scum.

"Oh, don't worry about it! Look at the outside of the bowl. See? Sparkling!" I exclaim with no concern. *Gross!* Isn't the inside what really matters here?!

Jesus told a group of people called the Pharisees that they were just like my dirty bowls at the dinner table:

> Woe to you, teachers of the law and Pharisees, you hypocrites! You clean the outside of the cup and dish, but inside they are full of greed and self-indulgence. Blind Pharisee! First clean the inside of the cup and dish, and then the outside also will be clean.
>
> —Matthew 23:25–26

You may have heard of the Pharisees. They were religious rulers at the time, and they were all about perfectly obeying the rules of God and letting people know just how perfect they were. They had a rule for every minute of every day—what to eat, what to wear, even how to wash their hands. They lived life in opposition to what Jesus taught. They "started with demand of outward obedience and righteousness, and pointed to sonship as its goal; the gospel started with the free gift of forgiveness through faith and of sonship and pointed to obedience and righteousness as the goal."[5]

What do you think this analogy of the dishes, clean on the outside but dirty on the inside, means about our life with God?

Why are we bored with God? We focus on doing good things, looking godly on the outside, and checking off our God to-do list, so obeying the King is a boring chore. But when we let Jesus change our hearts, then obeying the King in this new zip code becomes less of a duty and more of a desire. Living as a Kingdom girl becomes, as Dwight Edwards calls it, a "want" instead of a "should." And isn't a "want" so much more delightful and enjoyable than a "should"?[6]

Get real with your heart. Do you have hints of Pharisee in you—a faith that focuses on keeping all the "Christian rules" because you *should* instead of because you *want to*?

God wants to capture our hearts, not just our good deeds. Our good deeds are "filthy rags" to Him (Isaiah 64:6). This new Kingdom of God is all about a life lived like Jesus, out of a changed heart that loves Jesus.

From Duty to Desire

Growing up, the Lucado girls frequently had "dish duty." Mom would cook, then Dad and us girls would clean. I hated doing dishes! It was such a boring chore to me. But the older I got and the more I understood my mom's love and sacrifice for me, the more I *wanted* to do the dishes. I did it out of gratitude, out of love for her.

It was the same in my faith. For example, I never understood why I couldn't just do whatever I wanted with my boyfriend. It was a duty for me to stay pure and not go "too far." It was all about keeping the rules—not crossing certain physical lines. How far could I go before it was too far? But the more I spent time with Jesus—getting to know His message, His life, what He did for me on the cross—the more I loved Him in a relationship, and the more I *wanted* to stay pure because of my gratitude to Him, because of my trust in Him.

Bored with God? Then let me ask you this: Have you come to know Jesus in such a way that your love for and trust in Him are so strong that you *want* to follow Him, that you *want* to make Him king over your life? If not, what's holding you back from knowing Jesus in this kind of way? (Write your thoughts in the margins.)

A New Home

So we've thought a lot about the new culture of this new Kingdom. It's a culture that obeys God and lives for Him out of a heart that loves Him. But earlier I mentioned that when we move, we experience not only a new culture, but also a new home. To close out, I want to tell you about this new home in God's Kingdom.

I don't know what your home is like right now. Maybe you come from a broken home. Maybe your dad is distant or your mom is sick. Maybe you and your siblings are constantly competing and fighting. Maybe you don't know your parents or one has died. Maybe you are wealthy. Maybe you are barely scraping by. Maybe your home is happy, maybe it's sad. But whatever home you have now, know that this new home in the Kingdom of God is always warm, always loving, always at peace, always standing up for what is right, always positive, never changing, and will never fall apart.

God wants to capture our hearts, not just our good deeds.

It's a home that starts in your heart. Jesus is your foundation. With Him, you will not be shaken. No matter what storm blows through or how hard you fall, His love remains concrete. Instead of walls, God promises to come behind you and go before you (Isaiah 52:12). He has a hedge of protection around you. Instead of a roof, He shades you in the shadow of His wings (Psalm 17:8). The Holy Spirit fills the home—not with furniture or picture frames—but with peace, love, joy, kindness, gentleness, patience, goodness, faithfulness, and self-control. It is a perfect home. And God becomes your perfect family. He is the dad who will never lose His temper, the mom who will always comfort you, the sister you need to confide in, the brother who protects you. In this new Kingdom, your heart finally finds the home it has always wanted.

Just as Jesus wowed Capernaum, may He wow you today. May the message of a new life, this Kingdom life, send shivers up your spine. May the thought of God giving you a new home with Him send tears down your cheek. And may the thought of a life modeled after the Creator of life spread a smile across your face.

> **But he who looks into the perfect law of liberty and *continues in it*, and is not a forgetful hearer but a doer of the work, this one will be blessed in what he does.**
>
> —James 1:25 NKJV, emphasis mine

Going Deeper

When we read the verse above, we see James describe the "law"—which is another term for God's commands—as a "law of liberty." Liberty? How can rules be freeing? Isn't that an oxymoron? Earlier we chatted about God's rules going from duty to desire in His new Kingdom. Once you begin to walk in a life of obedience to the King, you will see that His way of living brings you a life of freedom, not a life in a prison of rules.

I used to hate my parents' rules! They didn't allow me to watch certain movies, hang out with certain people, wear certain clothes. I would try to break their rules. And every time I broke a rule, I thought it would give me that sense of freedom I so wanted. It didn't. I thought it would make me feel better. It didn't. I have to say, breaking my parents' rules did nothing for me but make me feel tied to a leash.

Leash? What do you mean?

Well, I became leashed to the dark parts of myself.

For example, I can remember lying to my parents about which movie I was going to see at the theater. They thought I was going to see a PG-rated movie, when I really went to see a horror movie that was rated R. Little did I know that after watching the movie—hearing the crass language, seeing the scary scenes—my mind would be filled with dark images and new fears that I had never had before, new scenarios that I hadn't thought possible. I was tied to dark thoughts. *One rope.*

During my freshman year of high school, I told my parents I was going to a slumber party, when in reality I was spending the night at my friend's house who was throwing a huge party. I was surrounded by people who pressured me to drink; so I did. I was surrounded by girls who defined popularity by breaking the rules, wearing tight clothes, and finding guys to "hook up" with, so I tried to live by those standards to gain more status. And when I got more attention for drinking, talking, and dressing like them, I wanted more. I was tied to popularity. Tied to the dark parts of my heart. *Two ropes.*

See how this works?

I always believed my parents' rules were stupid, worthless, and overbearing. So if I broke them, then I would find freedom, right? Wrong. I noticed that every time I disobeyed my parents, my heart became tied down—leashed to popularity, leashed to my appearance, leashed to my dark and scary thoughts. Turns out my parents' rules were actually to prevent my heart from being tied down by the world!

God, as our heavenly parent, does the same thing. We find His rules in the Bible. But these are not laws to weigh us down. They are laws that mold us to look more and more like Him, and when we live like Him, we find freedom and life like never before!

Write down some broken rules you thought would give you a sense of freedom, but which later made you feel more tied down.

Let's pray:

God, give me the strength to live in this new Kingdom. Make my heart Your home. Make it more like You. That way I will experience the unboring life You have called me to live through faith in Jesus. Thank You for Your Kingdom. Thank You for Your laws of liberty. Amen.

To Sum It Up

Why do we get bored with God?

We are in the wrong zip code. We are too focused on the exterior—following the rules. We haven't fallen in love with

Jesus in such a way that living for Him is a delight instead of a duty.

Knowing this, how do we get unbored with God?

We begin to get to know Jesus in a relationship so that our hearts will want to live this new Kingdom life. When we live in this new zip code, we live the freeing life God created us to live. We live a life like Jesus. And Jesus' life was *not* boring!

10

Praying about Praying

I've known Erin and Molly for a while now. They used to be best friends. Attached at the hip. But recently Molly has been frustrated with Erin. Erin has been distant, and Molly is confused.

Well, what Molly didn't know was that Erin couldn't take it any longer. It seemed that every time they hung out, Molly was crying about the same type of boy problems over and over. But anytime Erin would try to offer advice, Molly wouldn't listen.

You see, Molly has been "stoop dating." Do you know what stoop dating is? Typically, most girls have standards when it comes to guys. But when you throw those standards out the window and stoop down to a lower level to date someone who is far from your dream guy, that's stoop dating. Molly has been stooping low, dating immature boys. Every time she gets hurt, every time she runs to Erin for advice, every time Erin reminds her that these kinds of guys are not good for her, and every time Molly will not take Erin's advice.

See, Molly wasn't in a place where she wanted to hear. Because hearing often brings conviction, and conviction often brings change. And as much as these guys hurt her, she preferred the attention over the change. We all have a little "Molly" in us in our relationship with God, especially when talking about the word that we are going to spend this chapter analyzing—*prayer.*

A lot of times we make God out to be Erin. We run to God every time we have a problem, but we don't stop to listen and accept the advice, just like Molly wouldn't stop and listen to Erin. Prayer shouldn't look like Molly. With Molly, it's a one-way street. She wants to talk, but she refuses to listen.

Prayer consists of two voices: yours and God's. It's important to not only talk to God through prayer, but also to listen to Him through prayer.

Sometimes I think God must get so weary of me approaching Him about the same problem over and over. But He *never* grows weary of His children. He loves us too much. God will never be sick of you the way Erin grew sick of Molly. But to get the most out of prayer, it is important to examine the way we pray to God.

Why are we bored with God? Because we don't understand what a healthy prayer life looks like. When we pray the way the Bible asks us to pray, we will find a deep connection with God that shakes up our bored hearts. So let's talk about the problems we have with prayer and then talk about what prayer should look like.

What Should Prayer Be?

Often we think prayer consists of us crying to God over and over about our problems instead of taking the time to hear what He has to say about them. We don't stop to listen either because we don't believe we can hear Him or because we are too scared or lazy to hear advice from Him that might spur us to change.

Richard Foster says it best: "To pray is to change. Prayer is the central avenue God uses to transform us. If we are unwilling to change, we will abandon prayer."[1]

Stuck in a rut with God? Don't know what to do next, how to go deeper? Pray! It's through prayer that God can change your heart so that you grow closer to Him. You will be amazed at how He works in you and through you!

Prayer changes you to be more like Jesus. As you talk to Him, He talks to you, changing your mind to think more like Him, changing your heart to desire what He desires.

Pray about Praying

What keeps you from praying, or from praying *more*?

....

....

Life-changing prayer is not necessarily something that can just—*boom!*—happen overnight. In fact, I need to be honest and say I am *far* from where I need to be in prayer. Just today, as I started typing up this chapter, I thought, *How hypocritical! Here I am talking about the importance of prayer, and I haven't even stopped to pray over this chapter!* Sometimes we have to pray about praying! It's not always a natural inclination. It's something we have to ask God to help us with.

But I also don't want to scare you into thinking prayer is difficult. Prayer isn't some formula you have to master; it's just the process of a relationship growing. It's you getting to know God, and God showing Himself more to you.

Think about a close friend or close relationship you have. More than likely, even after you had hung out with this person the first couple of times, you didn't finish her sentences or know what her opinions were about recycling or how she felt about abortion. It takes time to know someone well. It's a learning process.

And so is prayer!

Richard Foster, whom I quoted earlier, offers some revealing insight on prayer: "Real prayer is something we learn."[2] He goes on to mention that the disciples asked Jesus *how* to pray.

"Lord, teach us to pray" (Luke 11:1 NCV). Now, if you think about it, it's not as if these disciples had never prayed before. They were Jewish. And in their culture, prayer was a daily part of life.

So for them to ask Jesus how to pray may have meant that Jesus prayed in a way they had never seen before! In a way that they wanted and desired for their own lives. Maybe it was their first time to see prayer so intimate with the Father. Maybe it was their first time to see prayer powerfully answered.

Do you want that? I do! I want a prayer life like Jesus. One where I know without a doubt that I am close to my Father, that He hears me, and that He will answer me.

Praying Like Jesus

So what should this praying stuff look like?

There's *no* way I can answer that question in one chapter! There are so many different ways to pray. We can pray standing up, sitting down, lying down. We can pray a prayer of thanksgiving, of confession, of intercession, of desperation, of declaration. The ways and words are endless! But let's look at some of the tips Jesus tells us in Mathew 6 about how to pray. (In fact, if you want to, go ahead and check out Matthew 6:5–14.)

1. Don't make a show out of your prayers (v. 5).
   Prayers don't need to impress anyone else. God doesn't appreciate us trying to look all high-and-mighty. If you catch yourself praying in a group and thinking more about what others will think about your prayers, then this could be a good Jesus tip for you to hold on

to. I love the way Matthew Henry says it. He tells us to not make prayer "a service of the tongue, when it is not the service of the soul."[3] That means, just pray from your heart! Don't worry about your words impressing God either. God is already impressed by you. He just wants some time with His little girl. No big words or fancy performance. Just you.

2. Find a quiet, secluded place (v. 6).
   Praying in a quiet place will keep you from distractions. Turn the cell phone off, turn the music off, go outside, or close the door. Do whatever it takes for you to be able to focus on God and hear what He wants to say to your heart.

3. Be yourself, your *whole* self (vv. 7–8).
   It's important to come before God completely honest. He already sees into your heart, so you might as well stop trying to act like everything is sunshine and cupcakes. God wants you to get real with Him so that He can get real with you. The more closed off you are, the more you close God out. Let Him speak to every part of your heart.

4. Picture God as a close Father, not a distant uncle (v. 8).
   It's important to know that God is a loving Father so you can feel completely comfortable in His presence. It gives you assurance that He is listening and cares about what you are saying. If we picture God as a long-distance number, wasting His time and money as we

talk to Him, we will never be able to enjoy His presence. He is not a long-distance call. He is right beside you. So sit and stay a while. There's nothing He loves more.

5. Trust Him as a Father (v. 8).
   As we pray to God, let's also tell Him that we trust in His best for our lives. Going to God with a five-year plan doesn't necessarily say, "I need your help"; it says, "Make it happen." God is bigger than you. (You probably already knew that.) But for some reason, we think we know what is best. Let's make it a point to go to Him with submission to His plan, even when it is different from our own. His plan always works out best in the end.

In Matthew 6:9–13, Jesus gives His disciples a prayer model. Go ahead and read it. Then, after you read it, take some time to underline certain parts of the prayer that you rarely pray for. Maybe it's the part about asking God to provide just what we need . . . no more, no less, just our "daily bread." Maybe you, like me, fail to praise God for how good He is while you're praying. See what line jumps out at you and underline it.

Our Father in heaven,
hallowed be your name,
your kingdom come,
your will be done
on earth as it is in heaven.
Give us today our daily bread.

Forgive us our debts,
as we also have forgiven our debtors.
And lead us not into temptation,
but deliver us from the evil one.

I've mentioned this before, but I'll say it again—if I am ever struggling with feeling uninterested in God, it's usually because I'm distant from God.

It's time to draw closer, girly. Closer to the God who wants to show you that He longs to talk to His girls, listen to His girls, and answer His girls. Did you hear that? The God who can hold the universe in His hand? Yeah, that one! He wants to hang out with you! And do you know what else? He wants to show off for you!

God shows off His power mightily through prayer. And this power will knock you on your booty, so get ready. Go ahead and read some of these awesome prayer stories that girls have sent me on Facebook.

Prayer Is for Real

Amber, Senior

I was sexually assaulted two years ago. I felt as though it ruined my life. But after about six months, I came to realize that God could use it for good. Not only did I have a better relationship with my parents, but I also got the courage from God to tell my story to three youth groups. One thing had bothered me still after a year. I didn't have the courage to forgive the guy who did it. A couple of days before the Revolve Tour—this cool all-girl weekend event—I prayed that something would be said or done to help me start the process of forgiving him. I still remember as if it were yesterday. Jenn Helvering, a speaker onstage, said, "Forgiveness isn't really for their benefit; it's for your benefit to move on with your life." I went back to our hotel that night and prayed, and within that weekend, I had forgiven the guy who assaulted me with the help of God.

Ashley, Senior

A year and a half ago, my best friend Emily asked me, "Why are you a Christian?" I was kind of shocked by the question at first, because I knew for a fact that she wasn't a Christian, and I'd never been asked the question before. I replied, "Being a Christian is like having a not-so-secret admirer. Jesus knows everything about you and yearns for you to know everything about Him. It gives you the butterflies sometimes." And she just smiled and said thanks. I kept praying for her, and a few days later she asked me to show her some Bible verses. So I did. A week later she came to youth group with me. And less than a month after that, she was baptized! It was so amazing to know that God used me to add one more person to the Kingdom!

These are *real* stories of how God *really* changes lives through a conversation with Him! Amber learned to forgive, and Ashley learned that God can use her to do great things. God never ceases to amaze me by how He hears our prayers and answers them. Bored with God? Try pursuing a consistent prayer life, and watch God work!

Going Deeper

Can't find the words to say in prayer? The Bible is full of words that you can pray over your worries, confusion, sadness . . .

I love to pray Scripture over my own life because nothing is more powerful than taking God-inspired words and using them as weapons to fight whatever problem, insecurity, or fear I'm facing.

> In praying Scripture, I not only find myself in intimate communication with God, but my mind is being retrained, or renewed . . . to think His thoughts about my situation rather than mine.
>
> —Beth Moore, *Praying God's Word*[4]

Read some of the following verses that apply to a certain struggle and then turn them into a prayer for your own life. I'll do the first one for you. Then take some time to write out your own prayers using the Scripture provided.

Struggling with fear?

> There is no fear in love. But perfect love drives out fear.
>
> —1 John 4:18

Cast all your anxiety on him because he cares for you.

—1 Peter 5:7

God, I struggle with fear of my future, fear of losing people, fear of failure. But You say that perfect love drives out fear. You are perfect love. So, God, drive out any fear in me. And instead of hanging on to the fears, help me cast them on You because You care about me and my heart. Thank You for caring for me. Amen.

Struggling with patience?

The LORD is compassionate and gracious, slow to anger, abounding in love.

—Psalm 103:8

But the fruit of the Spirit is love, joy, peace, patience, kindness, goodness, faithfulness, gentleness and self-control . . . Since we live by the Spirit, let us keep in step with the Spirit.

—Galatians 5:22–25

....

....

Struggling with doubt?

Then he said to Thomas, "Put your finger here; see my hands. Reach out your hand and put it into my side. Stop doubting and believe."

—John 20:27

[Jesus said,] "Everything is possible for him who believes." Immediately the boy's father exclaimed, "I do believe; help me overcome my unbelief!"

—Mark 9:23–24

....

....

....

....

We've talked about how Scripture is alive and active. Now, mix that with prayer and you get a powerful combo! It will show you how, through prayer, God really does move in your life. And seeing God move in my life has given me some of my biggest blah-to-awe moments.

Let's close now by asking God to help us get to know Him through prayer.

God, talking to You can be hard sometimes. Please help me learn how to pray. Help me believe You are listening. Help me hear Your voice. I want to see Your power, and I want my faith to deepen through prayer. Amen.

To Sum It Up

Why do we get bored with God?

We do not have healthy prayer lives. When we don't treat prayer as a two-way conversation, then we focus on our words and not God's. And anytime the focus is on our own lives, our faith in God grows dull. We aren't letting Him work in our hearts!

Knowing this, how do we get unbored with God?

We pray for a better prayer life. We model our prayer lives after Jesus' words in Matthew. We pray Scripture over our hearts and specific situations.

11

Strap Me In

The Deaf Teach Me to Hear

"What happened to this place?" my friend Sarah asked from the back of an old pickup truck.

"What do you mean?" James, our trip leader, responded.

"Well, it looks like there was a natural disaster or something. Hurricane? Tornado? This place looks wrecked!"

"No, Sarah, that's just what it looks like here," James said as he gazed out across the shacks and trash-filled streets with sad eyes.

Haiti.

A country devastated by poverty.

It was nine years before the 2010 earthquake, 7.0 in magnitude, struck the already-feeble country, so my friend had no newsworthy reason to ask her question. But if you have ever been to Haiti, if you had been with us in the back of that pickup, then you would have been wondering the same thing: *What happened to Haiti?*

Sarah had asked her question on an average Haitian day. The sun was shining, people were smiling, yet her assumption of a natural disaster was understandable. Because even without hurricane winds or earthquake violence, the country looks victimized. Sewage floats alongside the streets. And I'm using the word "streets" very loosely. Deep potholes, protruding rocks, and no traffic signals easily turn a normal fifteen-minute commute into an hour-long trip. The bay is a collection of bobbing trash, and all day long shoeless children who cannot afford to go to school, jobless men with downcast faces, and weathered women scrounging for food flood the "streets" alongside swine and chickens.

I was sixteen when I decided to join a group of students from my church on a short-term mission trip to Cap-Haitien, a northern city in Haiti. We worked with an orphanage for a week, living with the kids, playing with them, teaching them about the Bible, and doing arts and crafts. That short week changed me forever, but there was one night in particular that I can still see, smell, and hear in my memory.

On this particular day, our team traveled six hours into the tropical mountains to a remote village orphanage. We pulled up to a cactus fence, and waiting behind the thorns were the prettiest faces I had ever seen. The orphans were dirty and wore tattered clothes, but their hair was black and shiny, and their smiles were gleaming bright and white.

Interesting fact: Malnutrition is often noticeable in hair. In Haiti, the children who were protein deficient, in other words, just not receiving enough to eat, had a reddish or blondish tint to their hair. Black, shiny hair is often a sign of health.[1]

They smiled as we blew bubbles. They smiled as we painted pictures. They smiled when we grabbed their hands to play ring-around-the-rosy. But how could they smile? They had no showers, no rooms of their own, no parents, no movie theaters. Yet somehow their smiles were more sincere than any I had ever seen.

That evening we gathered in the church building—a simple structure with cement walls, small wooden chairs, and plastic flowers. We filed in with our pampered, wealthy, germ-ridden hands intertwined with simple, poor, dirt-stained hands. We sat down, and in our own languages we sang to one God. The voices were average, but the hearts were strong as our songs bounced off the cement walls and out into the quiet town.

Next to me sat a Haitian girl who had caught my attention earlier. The orphanage directors informed me that she was deaf. In a village where education is already scarce, the idea of sign-language instruction is unthinkable. So at nine years of age, this little girl communicated like a two-year-old, pointing and grunting. Now as she sat by my side, I watched as her head nodded and her eyelids got heavier. Finally, she surrendered to sleep in my lap.

As I stroked her cheek, I began to cry. This last school

year my mind had been consumed with prom, friends, guys. I had complained about not having enough snacks in a fully stocked pantry. I had whined when Mom wouldn't let me buy a cute top I thought I *needed*. And here I was with this little girl—who could not hear our singing, could not share her heart, could not even put words to what she felt. She would probably never have an education, a job, or a family. Did she dream? Did she know God loved her? My mind swarmed with conviction, questions, and confusion.

And that's when I heard God speak to my heart: *"The only way she can hear My words is through your actions."*

My actions? But God, my actions have been so self-focused! I must have misheard You! There's no way God could work through me, right? Wrong. That night God showed me an entirely new side of Himself—what He looks like *through* me.

If you hoard God's love, then you are bored with God's love.

I couldn't believe it! God could use my hands to touch His little girl. He could use my lap to rock His little girl to sleep. It was an overwhelming feeling of worth. God wants to use me—in spite of me! In spite of all my selfishness, complaining, greed, and spoiled American perspective, He wants to love on others through me. He wants to fill me up so high with Himself that His Spirit cannot help but overflow to others.

For one of the first times, I felt a surge of excitement about my journey with Jesus. I felt that same rush that you feel as you are sitting in the roller coaster car as it climbs to the top of the first drop. I told God I was ready for Him to strap me in for the ride.

Strapped In

We spent some time earlier talking about soaking up God's Word, praying, and having a relationship with Him in the new Kingdom. But now it's time to talk about what we do with all the love and peace and hope we soak up through Scripture and our relationship with Jesus. God asks us to spill out what we soak up. He wants us to share His love with others. And He wants to be the one moving through you so that you can be Jesus to others.

Have you done that?

Have you decided to tell God that you are ready for Him to work through you? Have you decided to take the love God has given you and spill it onto others? Because if not, God's love cannot be made complete in you. Look at this:

> If we love one another, God lives in us and his love is made complete in us.
>
> —1 John 4:12

If you hoard God's love, then you are bored with God's love. Until you and I get out and share who God is with others, we cannot experience the fullness of God's love in our own lives. There's another answer to our question. Why are we bored with God? Because we don't spill out the love God has given us onto others.

Sharing God's love doesn't mean you have to hold an orphan in Haiti. Although who knows? Maybe one day you will, or maybe you already have. But what are some ways God can love on others through you right now?

....

....

....

....

Serve Is the Word

One major way we can show others the love of God is through service. And because there are so many different ways to serve, let me give you a starting point.

Look at your strengths.

God has given you gifts, and when you take those gifts and ask God to help you use them to serve others, you can change the world. Pretty good idea, huh? Too bad it wasn't mine. Peter gives us this idea in 1 Peter 4:10. Look at what he says:

> **Each one should use whatever gift he has received to serve others.**

Stop and search your heart. What comes naturally for you? What are you good at? What do others affirm in you?

These are some good questions to ask yourself as you think about the different strengths and talents God has given you. Then write them down. (And remember, a gift doesn't have to be limited to a more stereotypical talent like art, music, or sports. You could be a natural at talking to people, hosting parties, writing encouraging notes, organizing, doing hair, fixing things, hugging, or telling jokes. Dig a little bit!)

Here are some examples from girls your age who have learned how to serve by using the gifts God has given them.

Josie

Josie has danced her entire life. She loves ballet and loves Jesus, so she started giving free ballet lessons to young women and girls at her church. That way, parents who couldn't afford lessons could still have an opportunity for their daughters to learn to dance. It also proved to be a great way to introduce families to church in a nonthreatening way. Josie taught her students that they could use their love for dance as a way to worship God. Josie's dance program grew from seven students during the first year to as many as 175 dancers!

Becca

Becca loves people—talking to them and hearing their stories. She decided to take her strong relational skills to the streets. She started a ministry in our youth group to feed and talk to homeless people. A group of students would meet at a house, boil some hot dogs, load up in some cars (with a couple of youth leaders, of course), and head to a poor area on the west side of San Antonio, Texas. There they passed out hot dogs and sat with the homeless, encouraging them, listening to them, and praying with them.

Katie

Katie loves to make cakes (and eat them). Every spring at our church we have a big banquet to honor all the graduating seniors. As a gift to all those who have supported her, Katie, a senior herself, designed and baked a beautiful cake to bless all of the students leaving, along with the church community who loved them. It took many hours to design and decorate, but that cake was gorgeous and tasted scrumptious.

Share the Word

Another way to spill out the love of God onto others is just by talking about God to others. I've noticed that after a conversation where I share how powerful the love of God is with someone else, the love of God becomes more powerful in my own life.

The other day I sat with a girl I have known almost my whole life. Her name is Jessica. She just finished high school and found out she is pregnant with her boyfriend's baby. She was lost. *Do I keep the baby? Do I abort? Do I give it up for adoption? How are my parents going to react to this?* These were just a few questions Jessica was facing.

When I heard the news, I asked her if she wanted to sit with me and just spill it—spill out her fears, frustrations, and confusion. So we met up at a coffee shop for some iced lattes, and I listened to her hurting heart. I've slowly learned over the years (and am continuing to learn) that the best hope I can give someone is not, "Don't worry. Everything will work out." It's not, "Hey, I'm here for you and will support you." Don't get me wrong. Those are kind words, and I still use them. But the best hope I can share is the love God has for them.

So I did. And the best way to tell others God loves them is by sharing with them the story we just talked about in chapter 9—the hope of the gospel and a place in a new Kingdom. I told Jessica why Jesus came and how His love has changed my life through a relationship with Him. I then told her that she could have a relationship with Jesus too. And although

Jessica didn't change in an instant and put her trust in Jesus right away, she thanked me for helping her understand God. She had never heard the good news explained that way before. She told me that what I was saying made more sense to her than the empty religion she had experienced so far.

Let me tell you, whenever I get to tell others about Jesus, it revs me up! It's as if I can feel God living in me, talking through me. It reminds me that He is so alive! And I don't know if you have ever experienced what it's like to feel Jesus alive in you, but it is this crazy-good-totally-exhilarating-I-can't-believe-God-just-used-me-this-is-so-awesome feeling.

Have you ever shared the story of God's love with someone else, or simply told someone else about how God has worked in your life? I realize it can be a little scary to share your faith with someone else, so take some time and write down your experiences and insecurities.

....

....

....

....

To be honest, sharing my faith—as great as sharing is—is not an easy thing for me. It takes courage. It takes the risk of being rejected. But when I do it, my faith is more than a feeling; it's alive! The story of God's love and His grace touches me in a deeper way when I see someone else hear it for the first time. When I feel spiritually dead, taking the time to intentionally seek out opportunities to share my faith wakes me up to how awesome God is! It's that roller-coaster rush I mentioned earlier. You strap in and ask God to take control of the ride. After all, you can't control the reactions of others. All you can do is ask God to speak and move through you. And what a rush it is when you finally let go of all the uncertainties and insecurities and let the Holy Spirit take control. And He will! The Holy Spirit never lets you go about it alone. Read this encouragement:

> Therefore go and make disciples of all nations, baptizing them in the name of the Father and of the Son and of the Holy Spirit, and teaching them to obey everything I have commanded you. And surely I am with you always, to the very end of the age.
>
> —Matthew 28:19–20

I love the promise at the end of this passage. What does Jesus promise here?

....

....

He is with you always. Know that when you tell others about Jesus, He is standing with you. He will give you strength. He will give you the words to say. And He will swell up with a smiling pride as you share the good news.

Sharing your faith is one of the scariest, most unsure steps of faith we can take, but it's a direct command from God that we need to obey. Todd Philipps talks about how God commanded the Israelites to cross the Jordan River to capture the promised land. Can you imagine stepping out in faith to do that? "Really, God? You want me to walk through that?" But Todd continues: "Yet, just as God promised the Israelites, as you obey he will part the waters of insecurity and fear, and you will stand firm in your witness for Christ. God's command: share your faith (Matthew 28:19–20). God's promise: complete joy."[2]

Going Deeper

The way you love others is a good test of how much you are allowing the love of God to fill you. So get real with yourself. Mark where you land on the love scales below:

I get into a "heated discussion" with one of my parents . . .

Daily Weekly Monthly Never

I have drama with friends . . .

Daily Weekly Monthly Never

I fight with my siblings . . .

Daily Weekly Monthly Never

Now, read the following verse:

> We love because he first loved us.
>
> —1 John 4:19

According to this verse, if you are struggling with loving people wholeheartedly, then what could be the problem?

....

....

....

....

....

....

To love others well, you have to know the love of God well. Only by *His* love can we serve others and love others in a way that makes faith exciting.

Let's close out by writing down other ways to spill out our love of God onto others, to love them with a God-love. Get personal about people in your own life. Maybe God wants to show you people in your life who are difficult to love. (Hint: More than likely a difficult person is living with you right now. Ahem, that sibling or parent?) Maybe God wants you to step out of your comfort zone and love on someone who would typically intimidate you. Yes, God calls us to love on the orphans and the poor, but it's just as important to start serving and loving the people in your own home and in your own school.

Let's pray about it.

God, I don't just want to love on the people who are easy to love. I want to love everyone. Would You fill me up with so much of You that Your love overflows onto everyone I encounter? Please speak to me now, and tell me whom You desire me to love more. And then give me the love to give them. Thank You for loving me when I'm difficult. Amen.

Write your ideas and thoughts here:

To Sum It Up

Why do we get bored with God?

Because we fail to share the love of God. And when we hoard God's love, we become bored with God's love. Why? Because we are not giving God a chance to use us and move through us. It's experiencing the love of God moving through you and onto another person that makes God feel so alive and so close.

Knowing this, how do we get unbored with God?

We look for opportunities to serve others, share our faith with others, and simply love others well. When we share the love of God, we experience God moving through us, and God's love is then made complete in us.

PART 2

Does God Care if I Am Bored with Him?

12

In the Beginning

Her Favorite Time of Day

"Mom, tell us again about your favorite time of day when you and Dad lived in the garden," the boys begged.

Every night the brothers tested new strategies to distract Mom from demanding bedtime.

"Okay, my loves, but this is it. As soon as I finish, you boys need to go to sleep. It's getting late," Eve said as sternly as she could, masking the smile underneath.

Since the boys were born, she had told them stories about the garden, describing the smells, the colors, the sounds, and the sights. Although it was impossible to paint a picture of the garden's splendor, Eve continued to talk to her boys about the home they never saw and never would. She hoped that talking about it would preserve its memory. But as the days turned into years, the garden memory grew faint, distant, as if it had only been a dream.

Her eyes began to mist.

Eve, get ahold of yourself. How many times do the boys see you cry as you think back to those days? It's your fault that they will never see it. Your fault, she thought to herself.

But more than shame, she felt far away—far away from the One whom she could never escape in the garden. Now she could barely remember the sound of His voice.

"Mom, are you okay?" her son Abel asked with concern.

"Oh, honey, you know your mom. I just miss it. That's all. Okay, where were we?" She quickly wiped a tear away with the back of her hand.

"We haven't even started!" Cain said with impatience.

Eve took in a long, slow breath, letting her mind go back to the place she would forever call home. A smile spread across her face as her mind drifted there.

"Oh, my sweet boys, I wish you could have spent just one day with me in the garden. Then you would have experienced my favorite time of day. Dusk.

"The sky slowly shuts her blue eyes as night begins to stir and the stars begin to blink.

"Oh, how I loved to watch the bright blue sky grow darker and darker until stars speckled it like freckles on a face." Eve brushed Cain's freckled nose, and he giggled. "But my favorite part about dusk was yet to come." The boys mouthed the words along with her. They had heard their mom talk about dusk in the garden their entire lives. It was a part of them. Every word.

Eve continued. "Birds nuzzle into nests. A cool breeze

tickles the trees, ruffling its leaves." At this point in the story, Eve always tickled her boys' tummies. They would brace themselves, knowing what was coming, but would still burst into squeals every time. Once they grew quiet, Eve began again. "I loved peeking into the nests—baby birds tucked under their mama's breast. But my favorite part about dusk was yet to come.

"The sun, always the star of the show, performs his final number, looking more brilliant and fiery than ever, leaving the flowers cheering 'Encore!' one last time before they fold their petals and sleep. The owls take their cue to hoot as they notice the moon moving to center stage.

"I loved applauding the sun's burnt oranges and hot pinks alongside the flowers. I loved the sound of the first hoot as a faint outline of the moon began to form. But . . ." Eve stopped and let the boys finish her sentence.

"My favorite part about dusk was yet to come!" Cain and Abel yelled in unison. Eve nodded her head, smiled, closed her eyes, and continued.

"It was this time of day that I would hear my favorite sound. A sound more familiar than the cricket song and more tender than the tickled tree leaves. My favorite sound of dusk was His footsteps as He walked through the grass, getting closer and closer.

"It was this time of day that I would behold my favorite sight. A sight more fiery than the sun, yet softer than the flower's petal. My favorite sight of dusk was His face, which I would spot from miles away as He walked through the grass, getting . . ."

"Closer and closer!" the boys called out together.

Eve laughed. "Why don't you tell the story? You know it just as well as I!"

"No, Mom! Keep going, keep going!" the boys begged, hiding their yawns. Eve knew it was only a matter of time before those little eyelids would start to sag, but she kept going.

"You see, sweet loves, those footsteps and that face belonged to the Creator—the Creator who said, 'Let there be light!' and there was. He spoke, and the world began. And because He loved us, the Creator would spend time walking and talking, singing and laughing with His creation. Can you believe it? *The* Creator wanted to be with *us*!"

If only I had known how much of a gift it was. What I would do—or not do—to have another evening with Him, Eve thought to herself.

The boys drifted into sleep, yet deep down Eve knew the story was more for herself than for her boys, so she opened her mouth and started again, "Every evening, at the slightest faintness of His footsteps, at the slightest faintness of His glowing face, I would run to Him. My heart would pound with each step, and the Creator would laugh, shaking the earth with joy. He would pick me up, twirl me around, and say, "*Oh, sweet Eve, how I delight in you, My precious creation. You are good.*"

As Eve recounted the words that her Creator spoke over her, she spoke them over her sons, fast asleep. "Oh, sweet boys, how I delight in you," she whispered.

And although the boys no longer listened, Eve continued the story just so she could feel that closeness to her Creator God again. It had been so long. She felt so distant from Him, almost cold toward Him. She longed to feel His love, that same excitement that she had when she ran toward Him in the garden.

"Adam and I would beg the Creator to tell us the story again. 'Tell us again about the time You formed me out of dust,' Adam would say. 'Tell us again about the time You formed the seas with all their fish,' I would plead.

"And although we asked Him every night to share the wonders of His power, He never grew weary of our request. He would open His mouth and start, 'In the beginning . . .'"

But Eve could not finish the creation story. Not tonight. Her heart ached too much and her throat closed too tightly for more words to come out.

Where to Start

In the beginning . . .

That's where you and I need to start.

To know if God really cares about how we feel about Him, if we are bored with Him, ever a little ho-hum in our faith, we have to go back.

And I'm talkin' *way* back. Further back than your grandma's "good ole days," further back than the days when men wore tights and girly wigs. Even further back than Cleopatra rocking the gold bangles. We have to go back to the story you just read. We have to travel back to the garden—the garden of Eden.

In the story, Eve is carrying a burden. This burden stems from the day she chose herself over God. Church people and theologians call this mess-up "the Fall." If you want to read more about it, check out Genesis 1–3, but if you want the abbreviated version, here ya go:

Adam and Eve: The CliffsNotes Version

Basically God gave Adam and Eve reign and rights over everything in the garden except for one tree. They couldn't eat from the Tree of Knowledge of Good and Evil. Well, one day, Eve—enticed by a serpent, whom we know as Satan—decided to eat from the tree and share the fruit with Adam. That's when everything went wrong.

When you open up a Bible, it only takes two pages for humans to mess up everything. Two lousy pages! My Bible contains 1,048 pages. That means that for 1,046 of those pages, we have a God who is trying to clean up His children's mess and show them (and "them" includes you and me) how life is supposed to look.

But before the Fall, in the first couple of pages, what do we see?

We see God creating the world.

We see Him forming man out of dirt.

We see Him giving Adam responsibility over a garden.

We see Him giving Adam a companion out of a rib.

We see Him saying that man and woman are made in His image.

And—this is the part I want to focus on—then we see God walking in the garden. Check out this verse:

> **Then the man and his wife heard the sound of the LORD God as he was walking in the garden in the cool of the day.**
>
> —Genesis 3:8

Did you read that? God walked around with man! He talked to them, listened to them, hung out with them. This is the verse that inspired "Her Favorite Time of Day." My imagination started swirling with pictures of God so close to His creation. What did His footsteps sound like? Are we talking loud, thunderclap stomps, or silently swift leopard leaps? And what did He look like? Was He just a bright light or in bodily form? Visible or just audible? I don't know, but as you can tell, it stirs my curiosity. If anything, this verse gives us a glimpse into who God is.

It implies that we don't have a God who is hard to reach, distant, or doesn't care. We have a God who stoops down to be with us, hang out with us, walk with us, be in relationship with us. He is up close and personal.

Bad-Breath-Messy-Hair-Comfy-Sweats God

Do you have a family member or friend who allows you to be totally, utterly yourself around him or her? You don't have to brush your teeth or your hair, change out of your comfortable sweatpants with all the holes, or say smart things. You know—the ultimate bad-breath-messy-hair-comfy-sweats friend. That's how I picture God. You don't have to impress

Him or clean up for Him. He is the ultimate bad-breath-messy-hair-comfy-sweats God. Why would I assume this? Probably because of Adam and Eve's wardrobe, or should I say, lack thereof. They were naked in front of God, for crying out loud! Nakedness, in my opinion, is the ultimate symbol of vulnerability. You are totally exposed. And yet Adam and Eve walked around with God, vulnerable, unashamed, and totally themselves.

So what does all this say to me? That we have a God who wants us to know Him, *really* know Him. He wants a relationship with you, a deep, intimate relationship—one that makes your heart race like Eve's did when she would hear Him walking in the garden.

> **In this way, we are made in God's image. Certainly God does not need people in the way you and I do, but He feels joy at being loved, and He feels a joy at delivering love.**
>
> —Donald Miller, *Searching for God Knows What*[1]

God's purpose behind creating relationships between you and a friend or sister or grandmother is not just about you getting to know another human being. No, even deeper than that, God created the concept of relationships so that we could learn more about *Him* and the type of relationship He desires with us. He loves it when we talk to Him, lean on Him, cry to Him, love Him just like we do in our relationships with our family and friends.

How do you think you learn about a relationship with God through a relationship with others?

....

....

....

....

I learned about the patience of God when my dad taught me how to drive. I learned about the concern of God every time my mom bandaged a wound. I learn about the listening ear of God when a girlfriend listens to me cry about my insecurities. God uses our relationships to point us to the kind of relationship He wants to be in with us.

So does God care if we are ever apathetic about Him, kind of okay without Him, even bored with Him? Of course! Why? Because He created us to be in an up-close and personal relationship with Him, and up-close and personal relationships aren't boring. They are constantly growing, ebbing and flowing, vulnerable, scary, insightful, and full of surprises, emotion, and passion. He didn't create us to be bored with Him; He created us to know Him. Not like you know your history teacher, and not like you know the pizza delivery guy. I mean *really* know Him!

> "You are my witnesses," declares the Lord, "and my servant whom I have chosen, so that you may *know* and believe me and understand that I am he."
>
> —Isaiah 43:10, emphasis mine

Think about the person you are closest to. Go ahead and write that person's name down in the space below. Why are you so close to that person? What is it about that person that allows you to be totally you?

....

....

....

....

Yadha, Yadha, Yadha

Go back to Isaiah 43:10. Read it one more time. I was studying this verse the other day, and Beth Moore, an author and speaker, gave me a deeper understanding that I want you to think about. She says this: "In Isaiah 43:10, the Hebrew word for 'know' is 'yadha.' The term reflected a personal level of familiarity and often depicted the relationship of a husband and wife."[2]

So what does this Hebrew word point to? A level of intimacy that a husband and wife share. And sure, you probably aren't married if you are reading this book, but it's cool to think that no matter if we marry or not, we can know true love and intimacy through a relationship with God.

In a relationship with God, He provides everything we

need, fills every hole, and satisfies our souls. He did in the garden. And He will today.

> **Our creation is by love, in love and for love.**
>
> **—Gerald May, as quoted in *The Sacred Romance*[3]**

God cares that sometimes we don't care about Him. He cares about how we think of Him, view Him, and feel about Him—and how we don't. He longs for us to be in a deep, "yadha" relationship with Him! And a yadha relationship is *not* blah.

Not His Idea

It was *never* God's idea for us to feel insecure, *never* His idea for us to have to suffer in this scary world, *never* His idea for us to feel dirty, *never* His idea for us to hide from Him, *never* His idea for us to feel distant from Him or bored with Him. But because of the Fall, God's ideal relationship with us was tainted as soon as Adam and Eve decided to reject God.

As soon as Adam and Eve sinned, they had something to hide. So what did they do? They made clothes to cover up their sin. These aren't clothes that you and I wear. We aren't talking togas or robes either. Read it for yourself: "They sewed fig leaves together and made coverings for themselves" (Genesis 3:7). All it took were a few fig leaves to separate us from God. For the first time, we see a wall distancing God from His beloved creation.

We were the ones who put something between God and us. And because of that, *we* are the reason we find ourselves spiritually apathetic. It's not God. It's us! He always wanted us to experience Him for who He is: a close, personal, loving God who meets every need in relationship with Him. Our need for love. Our need for acceptance. Our need for joy. But we've messed it up right alongside Adam and Eve.

Because of our flesh, we try to find value, joy, identity, purpose, and love in other people, in a shopping trip, in our number of friends, in our student council position, in the amount of points we make in a game. We reject God, telling Him that He isn't the answer. Telling Him we are bored with Him. And we move on.

Who do you go to, or what do you turn to, in order to find your value outside of God?

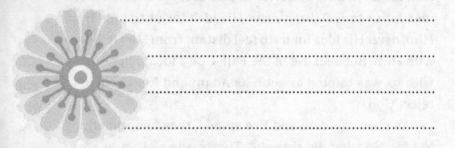

We find ourselves blah in our faith because we cannot fully experience the awe of God as God intended it to be from the beginning in the garden.

But God has offered a way out of our mess. Through Jesus, our sin that separates us from God is forgiven, and we can experience an intimate relationship with God. This relationship will not be fully restored until we are in heaven, but praise God that He cares about us enough to break through the sin barrier and strip away our stupid fig leaves so that we can draw near to Him once again. This act answers our "Does God care if I am bored with Him?" question with a resounding *yes*! He did whatever it took to restore an exciting, intimate relationship with His children—even though that meant sending His one and only Son.

Honey, you were made for more.

Made for More

Honey, you were made for more. You were made for more than the casual prayers you toss into the wind, more than reading a verse in the Bible every now and then, more than attending a church service. From the beginning, God created you to know Him in an intimate relationship, a bad-breath-messy-hair-comfy-sweats relationship. And that sort of relationship isn't boring!

Going Deeper

> **In some deep place within, we remember what we were made to be, image-bearers walking in the Garden.**
>
> **—Brent Curtis and John Eldredge, *The Sacred Romance*[4]**

God created us in His image. You may have heard that, but have you ever wondered how this relates to the importance of a relationship with God? John Eldredge says that before creation, we see God in relationship with the Son Jesus and the Holy Spirit. "The Trinity is at the center of the universe; perfect relationship is the heart of all reality."[5]

Because we were created in God's image, and God's image is a perfect relationship with the Son and Spirit, at the heart of who we are is a longing for perfect relationship. And the only place we will find it is in Him.

Let's look a little more into the type of relationship God calls us to. Read the following verses and circle any words that communicate the type of relationship God wants with you. Then take some time to describe those relationships. Are there any relationship analogies that comfort you, excite you, or confuse you? Write about them on the next page.

> I no longer call you servants, because a servant does not know what his master is doing. But I call you friends, because I have made known to you everything I heard from my Father.
>
> —John 15:15 NCV

> But Lord, you are our father. We are like clay, and you are the potter; your hands made us all.
>
> —Isaiah 64:8 NCV

Can a mother forget the baby at her breast and have no compassion on the child she has borne? Though she may forget, I will not forget you!

—Isaiah 49:15

As a bridegroom rejoices over his bride, so will your God rejoice over you.

—Isaiah 62:5

One day this earth will be restored to the way it was in the garden. This is the eternity God promises to those who are in Jesus. On that day, He will pick us up and twirl us around, just like He did with Eve in the garden. But until then, write down some ways you can strengthen the intimacy in your relationship with Him in this earthly home, and then pray about what you wrote.

To Sum It Up

Does God care if we are bored with Him?

Yes! He created us for the most intimate of relationships with Him. And within an intimate relationship there is emotion and passion. To see what our relationship with Him should look like, we go back to the garden of Eden.

Knowing this, how do we get unbored with God?

Boredom with God comes from the separation we have created; it doesn't come from Him. Knowing this allows us to focus our efforts on what is standing in the way of our intimacy with God, instead of blaming Him. Reading the Word of

God draws us closer to Him, and spending time with Him each day draws us into the beautiful love relationship He called us to be in from the creation of time.

13

God on Tour

Thousands of people file in, ticket stubs in hand, busily finding their assigned seats. Some buy T-shirts and glow sticks while others wait too long and pay too much for a stale pretzel and flat soda. But nothing can frustrate the people in this arena. They are all smiles as they eagerly await the moment the lights go down and the band walks out. A ten-minute countdown begins, and as the final seconds flash on the screen . . . 3 . . . 2 . . . 1, the crowd stands up and roars. A drumbeat starts the song, then the bass guitar. The electric guitar slides into place as the stage lights flash on. The crowd goes wild and then suddenly silent as the long-anticipated first note floats out of the lead singer's mouth. The arena shakes; people mosh near the front of the stage, while others dance in their seats.

Concerts. Why do people love them so much? Is it the blaring speakers that leave your ears ringing, the blinding lights that leave your eyes stinging, the crazy dancing that leaves your body sweating, or the loud singing that leaves your throat aching? Maybe you are more about the moving lyrics, the stories in between the songs, the perfect guitar lick, or the way he can play the piano so fluently and she can hit every note so effortlessly.

Do you remember your first concert? If so, take a fun minute and write about it.

Something had to attract the people who spent a total of $965.5 million on the top 100 tours in North America in the first six months of 2010 alone.[1] That's a lot of cash!

And something attracted almost 650,000 people worldwide to see a Taylor Swift concert and close to 735,000 people to see a Black Eyed Peas concert during the first six months of 2010.[2] That's a lot of people!

So what is it? What is it we love about live music? I can't help but wonder if it's this: There is something inside of us that wants to worship. We are a culture that loves to idolize, to glorify. At a concert, what are we doing? In a sense, we are idolizing a rock star and praising him/her/them or at least their music. Just the fact that we use the term "rock star" proves this deep, sometimes unrecognizable desire we have to put somebody (or something) on a pedestal.

Does that idea shock you a little bit?

Jenna! No way! When I go to a concert, I just want to have fun and enjoy the music.

And I'm sure that is very true. But let's think about it.

What are we doing when we clap after a song?

What are we doing when we scream as the band comes out on stage?

What are we doing when we are desperate for an encore?

What are we doing when we fight for the guitar pick thrown into the audience?

What are we doing when we tell all of our friends about the concert the next day?

We are glorifying a band, a band's music, an experience. We are a culture that loves to worship!

Need some more proof? Think through these questions:

Why are there Hollywood stars at all?

Why do some girls cry when they touch the sleeve of the latest heartthrob?

Why do people wear their favorite NBA, NFL, or MLB jerseys?

Why do you find yourself bragging about your favorite restaurant, store, movie?

If you're still not convinced, the fact we have a show titled *American Idol* says it all, in my opinion.

Again, use whatever nouns, pronouns, or verbs to answer the above questions any way you want, but the foundation for your answer will still be that we love to worship. So is this desire necessarily bad? Well, it is when we take God out of the equation.

And unfortunately, we have done just that. We've taken a God-given desire and made it selfish, glorifying ourselves or money or a cute boy or a musician. God put in us the need to worship, more specifically the need to "glorify" or experience the "glory" of Him. But because we messed everything up in the first two pages of the Bible, we have taken God's plan for us to glorify Him and warped it into worshiping the people or things of this earth. This is what God's plan looks like:

> **Everyone who is called by my name, whom I created for my *glory*, whom I formed and made.**
>
> —Isaiah 43:7, emphasis mine

In this verse, for whose glory were we created?

....

....

Does the verse say, "Everyone who is called by my name, whom I created to be bored with me, whom I formed and made"?

God cares how we feel about Him because He created us to honor Him more than any celebrity, be amazed by Him more than any intelligent mind, stand in awe of Him more than any rock star on a stage.

Throughout this book we have chatted about God creating us to be in an intimate relationship with Him. But it's important to know the purpose behind this relationship. Your relationship with Jesus is not, first and foremost, meant to benefit you. It's not, first and foremost, meant to make you feel loved and encouraged and all fuzzy inside. Everything in heaven and on earth exists first and foremost for the glory of God.

Your relationship with God, your attitude toward God, how you feel about God is *for God.* God created us to know His fame, wave His banner, praise Him front and center, point to Him, clap for Him, sing to Him, brag about Him. He created us for His glory.

What do you think that word, *glory,* means, anyway? We have plenty of books and movies that use the word, and if you go to church, you will hear it on a regular basis, but have you ever tried to define it?

What if I gave you a handful of Bible verses that use the word? Then you could start figuring out what you think the word means. In fact, I'm going to help you out even more and give you the verse in two different Bible versions: the New International Version (NIV) and *The Message* (MSG).

In the first verse, circle any form of the word *glory.* In the second verse, I've italicized the way *The Message* translates *glory,* so go ahead and circle the italicized words as well.

Sometimes when I don't understand a word, I look up its synonyms so I can grasp it. That's kind of what we are doing here. *The Message* version gives you a synonym for the word *glory* so that you can understand it in a deeper way.

John 13:31

Jesus said, "Now is the Son of Man glorified and God is glorified in him." (NIV)

Jesus said, "Now the Son of Man *is seen for who he is*, and God *seen for who he is* in him." (MSG)

Hebrews 1:3

The Son is the radiance of God's glory and the exact representation of his being, sustaining all things by his powerful word. (NIV)

This Son perfectly *mirrors God*, and is stamped with God's nature. He holds everything together by what he says—powerful words! (MSG)

Daniel 5:20

But when his heart became arrogant and hardened with pride, he was deposed from his royal throne and stripped of his glory. (NIV)

He developed a big head and a hard spirit. Then God knocked him off his high horse and stripped him of his *fame*. (MSG)

What did you find out about what *glory* signifies from these verses?

....

....

....

....

This is what I found out based on the verses above:

Glory = God seen for who He is.
Glory = Reflection of God. Jesus is the reflection of God.
Glory = Fame, reputation.

Is there an overall definition of *glory* you can come up with based on what we've discovered?

....

....

....

....

Glory is a hard word to define! Probably because it represents a God who is impossible to define. But this is my definition of *glory* based on the workings of my little human brain.

Glory is God showing off God. Glory is God making Himself known. Self-promotion.

It's all of His power, authority, brightness, goodness, awesomeness, holiness, righteousness, and any other "ness" word you can think of all balled up together. It's essentially just God in all His . . . Godness! I once heard a pastor call God's glory His "spectacularness."

Jonathan Edwards, a guy you may have heard of in history class, said this about God's glory: "God's name and His glory, at least very often signify the same thing."[3] So, for you math whizzes, if we were to put that sentence in an equation, it would look like this:

Glory is God making Himself known.

Glory = God
God = Glory

When we glorify God, that means we are showing others who God is through the way we live.

Moses Gets His Beard Blown Off

No one has seen the glory of God quite like Moses did. And I'm so excited to talk about this story with you because I can't get enough of it! It's one of my all-time favorite God stories.

Even after Moses witnessed some of the most famous miraculous wonders—plagues of locusts, the parting of the Red Sea, bread from heaven, water from a stone—we can still hear Moses saying this line that leads us into our story:

> Moses said to God, "Look, you tell me, 'Lead this people,' but you don't let me know whom you're going to send with me. You tell me, 'I know you well and you are special to me.' If I am so special to you, let me in on your plans. That way, I will continue being special to you. Don't

> forget, this is *your* people, your responsibility." (Exodus 33:12–13 MSG)

Doesn't it crack you up that Moses is speaking to God that way? Can't you just hear his tone? It's one I've used before when I'm unsure of someone else's plan. I want the credit if it goes well, but I don't want any blame if it all goes wrong.

Here we have Moses about to lead hundreds of thousands of people to a new land—the promised land God had given them—through a hot desert, with an entirely new way of doing life. This Ten Commandments stuff was brand spankin' new! And Moses wanted to make sure God had his back once he explained the new rules to everyone and temperatures began to rise. So God assures him, "My presence will go with you. I'll see the journey to the end" (Exodus 33:14 MSG).

But that wasn't reassuring enough for Moses. So do you know what he asks?

"Please. Let me see your Glory" (Exodus 33:18 MSG).

The first time I read this, I remember wondering, *What does that even mean? What will that look like?* The mystery of God's glory builds suspense. So how does God respond? In verse 19 God says, "I will make my Goodness pass right in front of you; I'll call out the name, GOD, right before you."

When Moses asks to see God's glory, what does God say? That He will show Moses His goodness and proclaim His name. So really God is saying, "I'll show you *Me*."

But, and this part I am so fascinated by . . .

> "You may not see my face. No one can see me and live."
>
> GOD said, "Look, here is a place right beside me. Put

> yourself on this rock. When my Glory passes by, I'll put you in the cleft of the rock and cover you with my hand until I've passed by. Then I'll take my hand away and you'll see my back."
>
> —Exodus 33:20–23 MSG

When I read this part of the story, I think of that old phrase "kill them with kindness." It takes on a literal meaning in this scene. God had to protect Moses from Himself because He is that good, that holy, that bright! Think about that!

Moses hangs out with this glorious God for forty days and forty nights. And when God was finished instructing him, Moses went back to the people. When the people saw him, they were freaked out. Do you know why?

> When Moses came down from Mount Sinai carrying the two Tablets of The Testimony, he didn't know that the skin of his face glowed because he had been speaking with GOD. Aaron and all the Israelites saw Moses, saw his radiant face, and held back, afraid to get close to him.
>
> —Exodus 34:29–30 MSG

After Moses spent every waking hour hanging out with God, God rubbed off on him. So much so, that God's glory shone all over Moses' face. And I'm sure his hair was a little windblown too.

And that's what happens to us when we get to know God for who He is—His glory. I'm not saying your hair will be windblown, but He makes you look more like Him. You begin to reflect God.

I guess that would be us *glorifying* Him—showing others God by the way we talk, make decisions, dress . . . live.

God . . . Live in Concert

Okay, so Moses witnessed God's glory, but how do we? Well, girly, I don't know if you've noticed, but God is constantly on tour. He is always putting on a concert, showing off Himself. God's glory is written in the stars, rises majestic in the mountains, and swells with the tides. God's glory is live in concert!

> God's glory is on *tour* in the skies, God-craft on exhibit across the horizon.
>
> —Psalm 19:1 MSG, emphasis mine

The best thing about this concert? It's free.

This concert doesn't need strobes or spotlights; God uses the sun and the moon.

This concert doesn't need a guitar or drums; God uses the song of the bird and the thumping rhythm of the people's hearts.

This concert doesn't need a stadium; God uses the universe.

This concert doesn't need graphics and special effects; God uses eclipses and shooting stars.

You and I can witness God through people we know, nature we see, songs we hear.

One of the best ways to encounter God's spectacularness

is through getting involved with a healthy church. When you see the church serving the community, you see more God. When you listen to the preacher talk about God's goodness, you are hearing more God. When you sing songs in church, you promote more God.

In all these ways, you are experiencing God's Godness, His glory.

In my own life, I have always experienced God's glory the most through worship music. I don't know if you think worship songs are boring or not, but nowadays you can find all kinds of worship music to fit your style. Get creative with your worship. You may think of singing to God as rigid bodies standing straight, holding hymnals. But in the Bible we see people dancing, playing instruments, doing all kinds of crazy things to make music to God. If you don't feel comfortable getting your dance moves on in a public place of worship at first, that's okay. But in your room, try turning on worship music you like and positioning your body to reflect a heart of worship. It may be kneeling, raising your hands, dancing. Each position can express to God a message of worship.

Kneeling = humility before God
Dancing = joy before God
Raised hands = reaching for God
Open hands = surrendering your life before God

Get outside of your worship comfort zone and ask God to show you more of Himself through worship.

Why Glorify God?

Now that we know more about what glory is and what it means to bring God more of it, I want to answer the questions "Why would God want to show off His glory?" and "Why did He create us to promote Him more?" Here is one of the answers I found with a little help from my dad:

> Think of it this way. You're floundering neck-deep in a dark, cold sea. Ship sinking. Life jacket deflating. Strength waning. Through the inky night comes the voice of a lifeboat pilot. But you cannot see him. What do you want the driver of the lifeboat to do?
>
> Be quiet? Say nothing? Stealth his way through the drowning passengers? By no means! You need volume! . . . You need to hear him say, "I am here. I am strong. I have room for you. I can save you!" Drowning passengers want the pilot to reveal his preeminence.
>
> Don't we want God to do the same?[4]

Without God, we are drowning. The Bible says without God we are as good as dead (Ephesians 2:1). And that's one of the reasons I believe God wants to show Himself off—to show the world that there is a Savior! And we are created to show off who He is, so that through our lives others can find that Savior.

One of the reasons God is all about promoting Himself is because He loves us.

Wait, what? How does that work?

Think about all that you desire—love, purpose, joy, peace,

life. Now think about where we turn to meet those desires—boys, popularity, family, achievements. . . . God knows we will never meet our deepest desires through things or people of this world, so what does He do? He puts Himself on display! He knows that *He* is the only one who can meet those desires, so by showing Himself off, He is pointing us to Him—the only One who will fill every need. He loves us too much to see us turning to the world for satisfaction. John Piper, a brilliant guy on this subject of glory, taught me this idea. He says it like this: "What could God give us to enjoy that would prove him most loving? There is only one possible answer: himself!"[5]

God didn't create you to be bored with Him; He created you to glorify Him. So of course He cares when we feel disconnected in our faith. He made us to experience His spectacularness!

Going Deeper

The Bible says, "Whether you eat or drink or whatever you do, do it all for the glory of God" (1 Corinthians 10:31). Can you think of someone who mirrors Jesus in the way he or she eats, drinks, talks, makes decisions? If so, write a little bit about that person and what specifically he or she does to show off God.

Is there an area in your life in which it is difficult to reflect God? Maybe a weakness of yours, a bad habit? Write about it.

....

....

....

....

....

The Bible asks us to glorify God in everything. When we do that we are also *worshiping* God. The words *worship* and *glorify* go hand in hand. You may limit the idea of worship to singing in church. But we can worship and glorify God in every part of our lives. It means we are honoring God and making Him the center of everything we do.

Write down how you can worship and glorify God in the following areas.

Doing homework:

....

....

Interacting with parents:

....

....

Playing sports or doing other extracurricular activities:

....

....

Now let's pray that God will help us show off His goodness more in our lives, making every area of our lives a way to worship Him.

God, help me honor You more with my words, my decisions, my relationships, my talents, and even in my weaknesses. I want to bring You glory in every area. I want to worship You with my life. Give me eyes to see Your glory more. Thank You for making Yourself known to us. Amen.

To Sum It Up

Does God care if we are bored with Him?

Yes! He didn't create us to be bored with Him; He created us to glorify Him!

Knowing this, how do we get unbored with God?

Through creation and through His people, we see just how amazing He is. It's a free concert that shakes more than stadium seats or an arena floor; it shakes up your heart, waking you up to how marvelous He is. As we live to glorify Him and know Him, we discover that our deepest needs are being met—our need for joy, peace, love, purpose, to be known . . . We find our hearts are fed as we glorify Him in everything we do. And this satisfaction is far from boring.

14

No Water, Texas

Mary-Margaret

She's only nineteen.

But she's lived enough life and made enough memories to fill fifty years' worth of scrapbook pages.

Though . . . her life isn't the scrapbooking kind.

Life used to excite her.

Every day a new day!

She wished every day could seem new again.

Now, no day's a new day.

Just a reminder of how far away from "new" she is.

Mary-Margaret is stuck. Stuck in the same town, same mundane routine, same bad reputation.

She can't remember the last time she was happy about something.

But she also can't remember the last time she was sad.

She is somewhere in the middle.

And sometimes the middle is the worst place to be.

Life is all dried up.

"Mary-Margaret! What in heaven's name are you doin'?!"

"Huh?" Mary-Margaret's head shook away the cloud.

"You are spillin' coffee all over the counter as if Bill here is going to lap it up like a dawg! Now clean that mess up and pay attention! You can't afford to lose this job. You know I'm only doin' it as a favor to your mama. If she was alive today, what would she think about the mess you makin'? Well, I bet . . ."

Mary-Margaret tuned her out. She's had to learn to tune a lot of people out. It's like changing the station on the car radio.

Rita is her guilt-trip station, and Mary-Margaret can only listen to Rita's song for so long before she feels so heavy she can hardly pick up her own foot. Sure, Rita had been good to her and all. But if it weren't her only form of income, Mary-Margaret would up and leave her job at the Sit-n-Sip Diner faster than ants swarm a picnic.

"I'm so sorry, Bill." Mary-Margaret wiped up the counter and served their most faithful customer a cup of his usual. Bill always came in wearing overalls and a long-sleeved plaid shirt no matter how hot the weather, and his lucky black cowboy hat, smelling of Camel cigarettes. Bill was as faithful as they come. Faithful to his oil rig job of forty years, faithful to his deceased wife of twenty-five years, and faithful to the Sit-n-Sip Diner for the last twenty-four years—a mid-morning ritual since the wife passed on.

Bill just nodded.

Mary-Margaret never has to change Bill's station because

he never has much to say except for "Mornin', ladies," or "See ya tomorrow."

Bill might be the only person I know who has a life more boring than mine, thought Mary-Margaret as she began slicing the pies and displaying them inside the glass case for the lunch crowd. She always wished she could look and smell like cherry pie. Shiny and tan on the outside, with a smooth, silky haircut that swirled like a dollop of whipped cream, full of sweetness. But her sweetness had soured, her dirty-blonde ponytail lacked any silky luster, and her freckled skin had aged with pain and paled because of the dark cloud that never left.

Bill is probably the only person in this town who ever speaks words to me that aren't hurtful, she thought. *Then again, he doesn't speak words that are particularly helpful either. I wonder if he knows what I've done?*

But the whole town knew.

Speaking of the whole town . . .

"Mary-Margaret! Here comes the lunch rush. You'd better have silverware on every one of them tables, or else you're gonna close tonight and open in the mornin'!" Rita yelled from the kitchen.

The first to walk in were the hard-hat boys: John, Ronnie, and Will.

In high school, they were always the loudest at the parties, the strongest on the team, and the dumbest in class. They used to be the most popular boys at No Water High School. After high school, they had switched out their football helmets for construction helmets.

They walked in and sneered over at Mary-Margaret filling up water glasses behind the counter.

"Hey, Mary-Margaret," Ronnie crooned as he leaned over the counter and let his gaze slide up and down her slim figure. "I got me my own place now if you want to come over later."

The other guys laughed and slouched at a booth with their legs spread. Mary-Margaret felt heat surge from the tips of her toes to the tops of her ears like a wildfire on a dry plain.

Just don't look at them, Mary-Margaret! she told herself firmly. *Why do you let them stupid boys hurt you still?*

If only she hadn't fallen for his sweet talk in the first place. Not soon after Daddy had left her and Mama with nothing but an empty bank account and loads of debt, Ronnie was the boy who had promised her the world.

"That ain't right that your daddy left you like that," Ronnie would say.

And I fell for it.

Fell like a dove shot out of the sky.

And I gave it all. All to him.

Only to be left with an empty heart and more debt.

Next to come into the diner were the church ladies.

Thelma and Ima.

Their white hair was permed into place along with their lives. They could never make a mistake, but could always tell you if you had.

"Well, hello there, Mary-Margaret." Thelma had a tight smile pasted on her face.

Ima ignored Mary-Margaret and immediately started whispering to Thelma as soon as they reached the corner table, the farthest from the counter.

Mary-Margaret hadn't been allowed to step out from behind the counter yet. Rita said it was because she would be a clumsy server, but Mary-Margaret knew the truth.

Because I'm dirty, people don't want me touchin' their food.

She couldn't decide if the counter was her comfort or her prison.

The noise level in the Sit-n-Sip Diner rose with the sounds of customers talking and dishes clanging. The door swung open again, and this time it brought in the worst of them all.

Counting up the change at the cash register, Mary-Margaret glanced up at the door and felt her stomach lurch as she caught a glimpse of the curly, bottle-blonde hair and heard the high-pitched giggles.

Not today! I can't catch a break. First the hard-hat boys, now them?

Mary-Margaret's heart—numb for so long—tightened with shame and grief and regret. She hadn't felt anything for such a long time. And though these weren't good feelings, they were feelings all the same.

She refused to look up and tried to make herself smaller. *If only I could crawl into the cash register and hide between the quarters*, she thought desperately.

The town called them beautiful.

Yeah, right. I guess if ya call backstabbers and gossipers beautiful.

In high school, they were the cheerleaders and had been on the homecoming court all four years. Their senior year, all four of the bottle-blondies had vied for the homecoming queen's crown. Of course, there's only one, so when Carla won it, the other three snuck into her room that very night and cut her bottle-blonde curls right off. The next day, Carla had walked into school wearing a bright pink straw hat to match her bright pink smile. Mary-Margaret had almost felt sorry for her—until she saw Carla walk straight up to the rest of the blonde bunch and act like nothing was wrong.

Mary-Margaret could see them sitting down at the window table, wearing their perfectly pressed, white summer dresses.

They had told her that white made her look fat.

Why did I ever believe them?

I believed them when they told me I could tell them anything.

I believed them when they told me Ronnie was a jerk for lovin' and leavin' me.

I believed them when they told me they didn't spread the rumor.

I believed them when they said Will was a good guy.

I believed them when they said sleepin' with Will would make him love me.

I believed them when they said Will would never leave me.

I believed them when they said Will was a jerk for lovin' and leavin' me just like Ronnie.

I believed them when they told me they didn't spread the rumor.

I saw the pattern too late. And by then, I was in too deep. I thought if I kept playin' their game, at least I would have someone to sit with at the lunch table. I should have known it was only a matter of time before the rumors started spreadin' faster than butter on a hot biscuit. My reputation was set. Might as well live up to it, right?

Mary-Margaret tried to change the station in her head, but their blonde song of betrayal was so loud, and it stung so deep!

"Hey!" Mary-Margaret was thankful for Rita's interruption. "Why don't you clean that bathroom? Those girls at the window table said it was dirty."

As Mary-Margaret walked toward the bathroom with her cleaning bucket in hand, she felt the blue-eyed stares and heard the high-pitched giggles of the girls in white.

She scrubbed as if she were scrubbing away all the memories, the rumors, the labels.

Daddy leaving without a single word.

Ronnie stealing the only valuable thing she had.

Then Will promising to love her different.

The blondes who gave her a lunch seat, then ripped it away, along with her dignity.

The rumors they spread.

Boy after boy she let climb into her window at night.

Boy after boy who slipped out her window early the next morning.

Mama dying.

And now . . . Corry.

Mary-Margaret stacked the paper towels higher and higher, building one excuse on top of the other.

He is the one guy in this dry town who doesn't judge me for sleepin' around. He lets me live with him for free. I got no money. No family. Where else am I supposed to go? He's older, more mature. He won't leave me like the others or sneak out my window like a burglar that just stole somethin'. Plus, I'm older now, more mature. Isn't that what two people do when they love each other anyways? And I love Corry . . . at least . . . I think I do.

She replaced the last toilet paper roll, but didn't want to leave the quiet sanctuary of the bathroom. She didn't want to face the judgment anymore. Shutting the toilet lid, Mary-Margaret sat down, hiding her face in her hands, until . . .

"Mary-Margaret!" shrilled Rita again.

"Yes, ma'am?" Mary-Margaret jumped and rushed out of the bathroom.

"Mary-Margaret, I'm gonna need to run to the store and buy a few more ketchup bottles. And I may just get me my nails done while I'm out. So that gives you no excuse not to have them tables bussed by the time I get back, ya hear?"

"Yes, Ms. Rita."

Mary-Margaret began wiping down tables and checking people out until finally . . . three o'clock.

By three, even the late lunch eaters were gone. Mary-Margaret straightened her slumped shoulders and at last dared to raise her downcast eyes to freely look around.

Just her, a dish towel, and some Clorox. Typically, this time of day reminded her of her boring, no-good, never-gonna-change life. But today she welcomed the silence.

In the middle of her deep cleaning and even deeper thoughts, the bell clanged as the front door swung open, letting in the dry summer air.

No one comes in at this time.

Mary-Margaret looked up to see a man she had never seen before.

"Hello there!" he said with a wide smile and eyes that twinkled kindly.

"Um, hi, sir. Are you here to pick up food to go?"

"Well, actually I thought I would come in and sit a while if that's all right with you."

It had been so long since someone had smiled at her, let alone asked her permission for anything, she didn't know how to respond.

Is this guy a joke? Did someone send him in here to poke fun at me?

"Well, sir, if you want a table, you'll have to wait till Rita gets back to serve ya. It shouldn't be too long."

"Actually, I was hoping that I could just sit at the counter, if you don't mind waitin' on me."

Mary-Margaret looked him straight in the eyes for the first time, shocked that he would want *her* to help him. Her lips parted, but no words came out.

"See, I'm on a long road trip," he said, "in a car with no air conditioning. And this Texas heat will leave you dry. So, really, I would love nothing more than a big glass of ice water and a chance to sit and rest in the cool for a while."

Mary-Margaret studied him. He was simple, wearing a plain gray T-shirt and a faded pair of jeans. He placed his car keys on the counter, along with an open bag of sunflower seeds. He sat down at the counter with an ease that somehow slowed down Mary-Margaret's anxious heart. And the way he talked . . . as if he had known her forever. Friendliest sound she had ever heard.

"Are you sure you want *me* to be the one to help you? Don't you know who I . . ." She stopped herself.

Mary-Margaret, stop it! Not everyone knows about your past!

"All right then, Mr.—?"

"Joshua. You can just call me Josh."

A simple name for a simple guy.

"I'll get you that ice water."

She grabbed a glass and the pitcher and began to pour.

The man with the kind eyes eagerly grabbed the glass she set before him and thanked her.

He took a long, deep drink. Then, with a satisfied smile, he said, "You know what I love about water?"

He paused, but she refused to look up.

"It sure does quench your thirst."

Does this guy think I'm dumb or somethin'? Of course water quenches your thirst!

She continued to wipe down the already-clean counter. And though she didn't entertain a two-way conversation, Mary-Margaret couldn't help but hang on his words like fresh laundry on a line. There was something about the way he spoke that felt like sunshine to her lifeless heart.

"You know what I *don't* like about this water?"

This time he paused long enough for Mary-Margaret to give in.

"What's that, mister?"

He waited until her downcast eyes looked up at him.

"The quench doesn't last. Not too far up the road here, I will have to pull my old car over for another glass of water."

He looked outside at the long, dusty road. His eyes turned back to her, and they were full of something Mary-Margaret hadn't had in a while.

Hope.

"But I can offer you water that will never leave you thirsty again."

Mary-Margaret's freckled brow furrowed with confusion.

"Is this some sort of sales pitch or somethin'? Because, sir, I ain't got no money to buy any of those energy drinks. I don't even like the taste really. You've come to the wrong . . ."

The man interrupted, "Margy."

Mary-Margaret's dish towel fluttered to the floor, and she froze in place.

She hadn't heard anyone call her that since her mama died.

Only the people who knew her, really knew her, called her Margy.

"Margy, I know your daddy left you. Then Ronnie and Will turned around and did the same thing. I know boy after boy has come and gone in your life, leaving your heart dry. And I know that you ran to Corry for the same reason you ran to the others."

Mary-Margaret didn't know whether to cry, scream, or call 9-1-1! *Who is this man?*

"You are thirsty."

Mary-Margaret's ears burned and her eyes stung, but for some reason, her heart tugged. She met his eyes and saw that she wasn't the only one holding back tears. But instead of giving in to the tug that threatened to spill open her heart, she snapped it shut like a scared clam. She hadn't opened her heart in a long time.

"Who sent you in here?" she asked in her big-girl voice, trying to mask her curiosity. "This is a joke, ain't it! Well, it's a mean one! Who do you think you are? God or somethin'?"

The man continued in his gentle tone without a single break, "Margy, it's time to drink from a pitcher that won't leave you dry again and again. It's time to fill your thirsty heart with the life you were made for."

Mary-Margaret stood still, not daring to move. If she did, the tears might tumble over the edge.

The man took a last swig of water and stood.

He smiled at her again. But this time the smile didn't startle her. It soothed her.

And the memories of her daddy, the good ones, the ones she had almost forgotten, came flooding back.

Daddy throwing her up in the air.

Daddy making her pancakes.

Daddy giving her Eskimo kisses before turning out the lights.

Daddy saying the three words that she hadn't heard in so long: "I love you."

"Margy, that's how I love you," Josh said, looking past her eyes and into her heart.

Then . . . she knew.

"Love me?" Her voice cracked as she let backed-up tears stream down her cheeks. "After all I've done? How can you . . ."

"Oh, Margy, my love goes deeper than Eskimo kisses and pancakes. My love is the water that you are thirsting for."

The man reached into his pocket and pulled out a business card.

"If you ever need anything, I'm just a call away."

He placed it on the counter, looked at Mary-Margaret one last time, and walked out.

Mary-Margaret knew it was time—time to live, truly live, for the first time.

Late that night when Corry walked up to the apartment door, he saw a note:

I'm gone, Corry. I'm leaving No Water. Time for me to learn how to really live.

Love, MM

Corry sat down on Mary-Margaret's side of the bed. Her stuff was gone. The room looked empty. He reached over to her bedside table, turned on the lamp, and saw the only clue she left.

A card.

A business card.

Living Water Corp.
Joshua, Founder and CEO
4John@samaria.com

Now take some time to read the real story. It comes from John 4:1–26, and it's one of my all-time favorites.

You can relate to Mary-Margaret, can't you?

You don't work at a diner in No Water, Texas, but you may know what it's like to feel stuck—stuck in a routine, stuck with a bad reputation, stuck in an unhealthy relationship, stuck in a feeling of hopelessness or purposelessness, stuck in what feels like a boring life. Mary-Margaret felt dead inside, dry of any joy. Maybe you have days like that, years like that. Not much joy, not many smiles, not much peace, not much excitement.

Throughout this book we have asked the question "Why?" to help us with those Mary-Margaret mundane days. *Why do I get bored with God?* Take some time to look back at the chapter sum-ups and write down some of the answers to our "Why?" question:

....

....

....

....

We talked about our hearts going against our made-in-China gods. We talked about not knowing the Bible, praying about praying . . . and the list goes on. But to sum it up in one line, we find ourselves bored with God because of sin in our lives. Sin separates us from Him and stands in the way of us experiencing life in Him and all He has to offer.

We find ourselves bored with God because of sin in our lives.

Hebrews 12:1 says, "Let us throw off everything that hinders and the sin that so easily entangles, and let us run with perseverance the race marked out for us."

What sin is entangling you, hindering you from experiencing a loving, intimate, and adventurous walk with God? What sins has God specifically convicted you of while reading this book? Write down those specific sins. Are they ones we discussed in this book—feeling embarrassed about living for God, not giving the Bible a chance, not obeying God, or not loving others with the love of God?

My prayer is that God helps you break down the walls, the bad habits, the pride—whatever it is that is keeping you from letting Him totally invade your life. If anything, my prayer is that when you read this last page coming up, you aren't okay. You aren't okay with where you are with God. You want more. You start to seek more. So many of us just go through a mundane walk with God, thinking that there is nothing more to life, nothing more to our relationships with Him. We settle for staying behind the Sit-n-Sip Diner counters, when God is exclaiming, "I didn't create you for this! Wake up! You have a life in Me that is full, so full, but you refuse to live it!" (John 10:10).

In the story of the Samaritan woman (the real Mary-Margaret), Jesus tells her that if she knew who it was that was asking her for a drink, "[she] would have asked him and he would have given [her] living water" (John 4:10). What does this "living water" mean? What does this "full life" mean that Jesus promises in John 10:10? Write down your thoughts.

....

....

....

....

Read the following verses and see if they influence your answer.

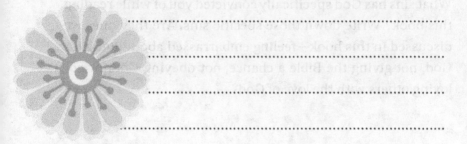

> **Your old life is dead. Your new life, which is your real life—even though invisible to spectators—is with Christ in God. He is your life.**
>
> —Colossians 3:3 MSG

> **The Spirit is life.**
>
> —Romans 8:6

According to these verses, who is your life? It's Jesus and His Spirit within you. At the end of this book, that's all I want you to remember. If you want life—life abundant, life that is adventurous and far from boring—then turn to Jesus.

The life He will give you isn't promised health, promised wealth, or a problem-free life. No. It's even better. It's a promise that the sunset painter, birdsong conductor, and mountain molder is with you in every moment of every day.

And knowing this can turn our everyday boring lives into everyday chances to sit in His presence and to share His presence with others. Through this, you experience the life you were made for.

> To incorporate God's presence in life's routine is the highest goal of the Christian . . . To think of Christ in the monotonous times, to yearn and burn for Him in the boring times—these become our tenderest moments . . . that's where our brokenness meets His beauty and the sum of our pain meets the power of His purpose.[1]

Every answer to our "How?" question—*How do I get unbored with God?*—points to an area in our lives that will help us spend time in the presence of Jesus and help share His presence with others. So now go back to the sum-ups and write out some of your "How?" answers.

....

....

....

....

And the final question we chatted about was, "Does God care if I'm bored with Him?" To that answer we have found a resounding *yes*! Yes, God cares, because He created you for more. Just like Joshua tells Mary-Margaret that His love is the water her dry soul is thirsting for, God responds to our dry faith and says, "You aren't drinking the right water if your faith is dull!" If you drink of Jesus—His love, His peace, His promises, His truth, His power—then your faith will go from a slow drip to a gushing spring.

So will you let Him? Will you let Him take your everyday blah faith and make it an everyday awe faith? Will you let Him shake you up? To close the curtain, I have written one last prayer that you and I can pray each morning. It's a prayer based on these chapters we have journeyed through together. Feel free to cut it out and tape it to your bathroom mirror, so that every day you are reminded to make each moment a God moment.

> *God, today I choose not to settle for a lifeless faith. And because of that decision . . .*
>
> *I hand my heart to You.*
>
> *I ask that You would take out any dark parts that are getting in the way of You and me. I ask that You would shape it to look more like Your Son's.*
>
> *Please help me not to get lost in the world in front of me. Instead, help me to live for the world beyond me. I pray that I will not serve a god I create in my mind, but that I will take every chance to get to know You, the true God. Help me step out of my comfort zone and stand up for You even when it's hard.*
>
> *Surprise me today, God! I want to learn something new about You—through a relationship, through a class, through nature—so that I don't ever feel like I have mastered*

You. Give me the diligence to read Your Word today, Lord, and may it change me.

Thank You for the gospel story. Thank You for saving me. May I never take that for granted. Today, help me live my life for You. Rule my heart so that my actions look more and more like the King's.

Remind me to talk to You throughout my day, God, to pray fervently so that You are a part of every interaction, every moment. Give me the courage and strength to love others as You love me, serve others as You came to serve, and share Your truth in a world that has lost truth. Give me the desire to obey You with a heart that trusts Your will over my own.

Thank You for loving me so much that You want a relationship with me. In everything I do, may I glorify You. I love You. Amen.

Notes

Chapter 2: Behind the Stage, Between the Lines, Beneath the Makeup

1. Stephen Smith, "When Do Children Stop Being Selfish?" *CBS News Healthwatch Online*, June 21, 2010, http://www.cbsnews.com/stories/2008/08/27/health/webmd/main4389606.shtml.
2. Dwight Edwards, *Revolution Within: A Fresh Look at Supernatural Living* (New York: Random House Digital, Inc., 2001), 5.

Chapter 3: Bored Makes Sense

1. Kaiser Family Foundation, "Generation M2: Media in the Lives of 8- to 18-Year-Olds," http://www.kff.org/entmedia/upload/8010_AppendixC_Toplines.pdf.
2. Martin Lindström and Philip Kotler, *Brand Sense: Sensory Secrets Behind the Stuff We Buy* (New York: Free Press, 2005), 16.
3. Ibid., 15.
4. John Eldredge, *Waking the Dead* (Nashville: Thomas Nelson, 2006), 28.
5. C. S. Lewis, *The Weight of Glory* (New York: HarperCollins, 1980), 46.
6. C. S. Lewis, *The Screwtape Letters* (New York: HarperCollins, 1996), 30.
7. Francis Chan, *Forgotten God: Reversing Our Tragic Neglect of the Holy Spirit* (Colorado Springs: David C. Cook, 2009), 34.

Chapter 4: Made-in-China God

1. YWCA, "Beauty at Any Cost: A YWCA Report on the Consequences of America's Beauty Obsession on Women and Girls," August

2008, http://www.ywca.org/atf/cf/%7B711d5519-9e3c-4362-b753-ad138b5d352c%7D/BEAUTY-AT-ANY-COST.PDF.
2. A. W. Tozer, *The Knowledge of the Holy: The Attributes of God: Their Meaning in the Christian Life* (New York: HarperOne, 1978), 1.

Chapter 5: Comfy, Cozy, Curled Up

1. Richard Wurmbrand, *Tortured for Christ* (Nashville: Thomas Nelson, 1998), 37–38.
2. DC Talk and The Voice of the Martyrs, *Jesus Freaks: Stories of Those Who Stood for Jesus—the Ultimate Jesus Freaks* (Tulsa: Albury Publishing, 1999).
3. Wurmbrand, *Tortured for Christ*, 37–38.
4. Oswald Chambers, *My Utmost for His Highest*, (Ulrichsville, OH: Barbour, 1963), 224.
5. Ramond B. Dillard and Tremper Longman III, *An Introduction to the Old Testament* (Grand Rapids, MI: Zondervan, 1994).
6. Mary Pipher, *Reviving Ophelia: Saving the Selves of Adolescent Girls* (New York: Putnam, 1994), 67–68.
7. Ginny Olson, *Teenage Girls: Exploring Issues Adolescent Girls Face and Strategies to Help Them* (Grand Rapids, MI: Zondervan, 2006), 191.
8. Rick Warren, "Reigniting Your Passion for God," sermon for Sunday, October 5, 2008, http://godswordonline.net/october52008.htm.
9. Ibid.

Chapter 6: Toss the Cap and Gown

1. Sean Dunn, *Bored with God: How Parents, Youth Leaders and Teachers Can Overcome Student Apathy* (Nottingham, UK: Inter-Varsity, 2004), 101.
2. Malcolm McLeon, *A Comfortable Faith* (New York: F. H. Revell Company, 1908), 22.

Chapter 7: Pruny Hearts

1. Pascal Folly, "Hope for Widows in India: Empowering Women and Girls Through God's Word," *Record Online, Digital Magazine of the*

American Bible Society, Winter 2010, http://record.americanbible.org/content/around-world/hope-widows-india.

2. Jill McGivering, "India's Neglected Widows," *BBC News Online*, February 2, 2002, http://news.bbc.co.uk/2/hi/south_asia/1795564.stm.
3. Pascal Folly, "Hope for Widows in India."
4. Library of Congress, "Everyday Mysteries: Fun Science Facts from the Library of Congress," October 13, 2010, http://www.loc.gov/rr/scitech/mysteries/wrinkles.html.
5. "Prune," *Merriam-Webster Online Dictionary*, Merriam-Webster, Inc., 2011, http://www.merriam-webster.com/dictionary/prune.

Chapter 8: A Very *Un*boring Story

1. Brent Curtis and John Eldredge, *The Sacred Romance: Drawing Closer to the Heart of God* (Nashville: Thomas Nelson, 1997), 39.
2. Ibid., 46.

Chapter 9: A New Zip Code

1. Donald English, *The Message of Mark* (Leicester, UK: InterVarsity Press, 1992), 54.
2. Eugene H. Peterson, *Conversations: The Message with Its Translator* (Colorado Springs: NavPress, 2001).
3. The XP3 Student Team, "Upside Down" (Session 1, "Collision," 9), XP3, http://whatisorange.org/xp3students/.
4. J. Alec Motyer, *The Message of James*, The Bible Speaks Today, ed. John R. W. Stott (Leicester, UK: InterVarsity, 1984), 70.
5. Alfred Edersheim, *The Life and Times of Jesus the Messiah* (New York: Longmans, Green & Co., 1896), 1:106.
6. Dwight Edwards, *Experiencing Christ Within: Passionately Embracing God's Provisions for Supernatural Living* (Colorado Springs: WaterBrook Press, 2002), 5.

Chapter 10: Praying about Praying

1. Richard Foster, *Celebration of Discipline: The Path to Spiritual Growth* (New York: Harper Collins, 1988), 117.
2. Ibid.

3. Matthew Henry, "Matthew 6:5," *Matthew Henry's Whole Bible Commentary*, http://biblecommenter.com/matthew/6-5.htm.
4. Beth Moore, *Praying God's Word: Breaking Free from Spiritual Strongholds* (Nashville: B&H Publishing Group, 2009), 8.

Chapter 11: Strap Me In

1. Neil K. Kaneshiro, "Kwashiorkor," *MedlinePlus*, http://www.nlm.nih.gov/medlineplus/ency/article/001604.htm.
2. Todd Phillips, *Spiritual CPR: Reviving a Flat-Lined Generation* (Colorado Springs, CO: Cook Communications Ministries, 2005), 85.

Chapter 12: In the Beginning

1. Donald Miller, *Searching for God Knows What* (Nashville: Thomas Nelson, 2004), 67.
2. Beth Moore, *Breaking Free: Discover the Victory of Total Surrender* (Nashville: B&H Publishing Group, 2007), 34.
3. Curtis and Eldredge, *The Sacred Romance*.
4. Ibid., 95.
5. John Eldredge, *Knowing the Heart of God* (Nashville: Thomas Nelson, 2009) 37.

Chapter 13: God on Tour

1. Jay Smith, "2010 By the Numbers (So Far)," *Pollstar: The Concert Hotwire*, July 9, 2010, http://www.pollstar.com/blogs/news/archive/2010/07/09/731238.aspx.
2. Ibid.
3. John Piper, *God's Passion for His Glory: Living the Vision of Jonathan Edwards* (Wheaton, IL: Crossway Books, 1998), 219.
4. Max Lucado, *It's Not About Me: Rescue from the Life We Thought Would Make Us Happy* (Nashville: Thomas Nelson, 2004), 30.
5. John Piper, *Desiring God: Meditations of a Christian Hedonist*, rev. ed. (Colorado Springs: Multnomah Books, 2011), 48.

Chapter 14: No Water, Texas

1. Christian George, *Godology: Because Knowing God Changes Everything* (Chicago: Moody Publishers, 2009) 153.

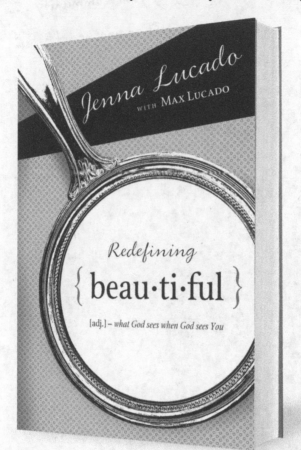

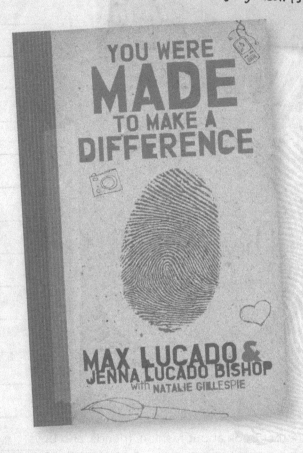